Lisbon

120th anniversary
Berlitz

W9-CIP-970

- A 🖙 in the text denotes a highly recommended sight
- A complete A–Z of practical information starts on p.104
- Extensive mapping on cover flaps

Berlitz Publishing Company, Inc.

Princeton   Mexico City   Dublin   Eschborn   Singapore

Text:	Martin Gostelow
Editors:	Donald Greig, Lemisse Al-Hafidh
Layout:	Media Content Marketing, Inc.
Photography:	Claude Hüber
Cartography:	Visual Image

Thanks to ENATUR, the Portuguese National Tourist Office in London and Lisbon for their kind assistance in thepreparation of this guide.

Found an error we should know about? Our editor would be happy to hear from you, and a postcard would do. Although we make every effort to ensure the accuracy of all the information in this book, changes do occur.

Cover photograph: *Torre de Belém*

ISBN 2-8315-6559-6
Revised 1997 – Second Printing May 1998

Printed in Switzerland by Weber SA, Bienne
029/805 RP

CONTENTS

Fact Sheets

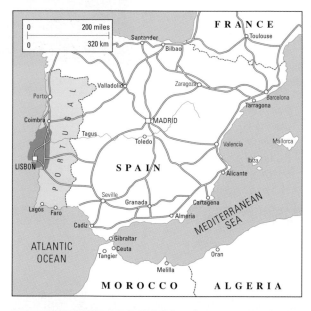

LISBON

LISBON AND
THE LISBOÊTAS

In a world of extremes, Lisbon steers for the happy medium. Don't expect to find the widest plaza or tallest cathedral ever built; extravagant claims are few here. Instead, the superlatives are in the people themselves, who are amongst the most dignified and compassionate you're likely to meet, as well as the most modest.

With a keen eye for beauty, the Lisboêtas decorate their balconies with flower pots, the walls with patterned tiles, the sidewalks with mosaics. At the bakery, old women all in black fill up their brightly decorated bread bags with oven-warm rolls. Any neighbourhood park keeps a few swans or ducks as pets, while in the bigger ones peacocks squat in the trees or strut across your path.

Lisbon is a city of hills and vantage-points – not seven hills as the legend claims, but nearly two dozen – and each offers a new perspective over the rows of tiled roofs and the magnificent harbour.

Here the Tagus River nears the end of its winding journey from the mountains of eastern Spain, swelling into what is known as the Straw Sea (the sun casts golden, straw-like reflections on the wide waters). Passing Lisbon, the river narrows sufficiently to be spanned by one of those rare local record breakers, the longest suspension bridge in Europe after it opened in 1966. From here the Tagus flows to meet the ocean, as did the daring explorers when they sailed from here in the 15th and 16th centuries to found the farthest-flung empire of the age.

Although the Atlantic lies only a few miles down the estuary, the climate is more like the Mediterranean. Mild winters and the city's sheltered, south-facing location result in the fact that palm trees and bird-of-paradise flowers flourish, and the balmy weather encourages an unhurried pace in this capital of nearly one million inhabitants. There is always plenty of time to pause for a cup of coffee and watch the various peoples from Portugal's glorious, imperial past, from Mozambique, Goa, Cape Verde, Macau or Angola, all mingling together and speaking in Portuguese.

Though the history of Lisbon goes back at least 3,000 years, the range of its ancient monuments is quite limited. One reason is the cataclysmic earthquake which destroyed many churches and palaces in 1755. A survivor is the Castelo de São Jorge (the Castle of St George) at the top of Lisbon's highest hill; it was begun by the Visigoths and expanded by the Moors. As you walk along its forbidding battlements you will appreciate the determination of the crusaders who captured it in 1147 after a siege lasting four months. The ramparts now protect a quiet park inhabited by pink flamingos, black ravens and white deer.

Almost everywhere you will see evidence – mostly circumstantial – of Lisbon's distant past: the Phoenician profile of the modern fishing boats; the Moorish expertise with painted tiles; the dark eyes of the people. Listen to their music, the *fado*, and ponder the timeless cry of longing and lament.

The *fado* is most at home in Lisbon's oldest neighbourhood, Alfama, where the soft strains of music can be heard night and day up and down the steep, winding streets. Filtering through the windows of medieval tenements, the saddest of songs may come from a radio or record player, or spontaneously in the voices of the local women and children.

A drastically less musical sound in this quarter is the piercing chant advertising the seafood specials of the day – the piercing caterwauling that helped to give fishwives a bad

*Lisbon is a haphazard mixture of elegance
and chaos scattered across the hillsides.*

name. The Alfama area can only be seen on foot, for many
streets are actually flights of steps, and the rest far too narrow for anything but a donkey cart, or much too steep for any
wheeled vehicle.

At the other end of the scale, Lisbon's central boulevard is
wide enough for 12 traffic lanes and even a couple of park-
ways. The Avenida da Liberdade, more than a century old, is
often likened to the Champs-Elysées in Paris – except that
the Lisbon version has palm trees, mosaic pavements and
duck ponds.

Elegant avenues and hilly alleys alike used to suffer from a
very particular problem: the walls were often defaced by political graffiti and posters. As soon as they were erased, then
new slogans were scrawled in their place, or occasionally
painted artistically, with the demands of political parties and
factions who had been unaccustomed to the right of free
speech. This phenomenon dated back to the revolution of
1974 which overthrew Portugal's long-standing dictatorship

After sorting out the washing (above), relax down at the beach (right).

and continued for years afterwards. However, political graffiti are no longer allowed by law, and the remnants are fast disappearing as buildings are cleaned or repainted.

It's easy to get along with the Lisboêtas, especially if you try to speak a couple of words of Portuguese. (If you manage a whole sentence they won't believe it.) Ask for directions and they will make sure you don't go astray; everyone will treat you with kindness and hospitality. The Lisboêtas are an unassuming people with a moderate nature and yet, theirs is a proud character of deep feeling and patriotism.

Sightseeing in Lisbon runs to monuments and parks, museums and churches – with a few surprises. The celebrated Tower of Belém, the landmark searched for by Portuguese explorers as they came home, turns out to be about half the size you expected. The stately church of São Vicente de Fora has a double-decker cloister lined with *azulejos* (painted tiles), which depict startlingly unmeditative scenes of hunting, sailing and the *Fables* of La Fontaine.

Though you would expect to see museums of Portuguese history and art, you will also discover an array of international masterpieces assembled in a perfect Lisbon setting by the Armenian oil billionaire, Calouste Gulbenkian.

You will want to get out of town, too, to take advantage of

the beautiful green countryside and the long beaches. A half-hour train ride takes you to the resorts of Estoril and Cascais, on the Costa do Estoril west of Lisbon, where after a day by the sea, you can visit the busy nightclub and roulette tables at the Estoril Casino.

For more pastoral pleasures, head for Sintra, known as one of the most charming towns in Europe. Even closer to Lisbon, the Versailles-style palace at Queluz is a 'must' – unless a visiting head of state happens to be there, when it is closed to the public. Alternatively, go on the cheapest excursion of all – a ferryboat to the south bank of the Tagus. You'll enjoy the excitement of the busy harbour and the enchanting views of Lisbon, and once across, yet another fascinating region of beaches, vineyards and windmills stretches before you.

In your travels you will also have plenty of opportunity to try the cuisine and discover the local specialities: fresh fish, seafood, fruit, vegetables and soups hearty enough for a tired sailor's homecoming. Almost every town seems to have its own particular dessert, each one sweeter than the next. As to Portugal's wines, they are as unpretentious as the people, and just as memorable.

A BRIEF HISTORY

Of all the legends surrounding Lisbon's birth, the most popular identifies Ulysses as the founding father. Hard-headed historians are more inclined to date the city's origins around 1200 BC, with the establishment of a Phoenician trading station. Its name was probably Alis Ubbo or Olissipo.

Primitive people had settled in the area thousands of years before, tempted by its location on a calm river close to the sea. Around 700 BC, Celtic tribes moved into northern and central Portugal, and the coastal settlements became part of the empire of Carthage.

Recorded history begins in 205 BC, when the Romans ousted the Carthaginians and created the province of Lusitania, though not without fierce resistance from the Celts. Lisbon was proclaimed a municipality and Julius Caesar is said to have named it Felicitas Julia – literally, 'Julius' Joy'.

The Romans introduced the growing of grapes, wheat and olives, built roads and also bequeathed the basis of the Portuguese language. As Roman power grew weaker the Iberian peninsula was overrun by Vandals and other Barbarians from north of the Pyrenees. Lisbon fell at the beginning of the 5th century, after which a succession of migratory tribes controlled the city until the arrival of the Visigoths in the 6th century, who provided a welcome period of peace.

The Moorish Conquest

During the year 711 a great Moslem invasion fleet from North Africa crossed the Strait of Gibraltar and within a few years conquered almost all of Iberia. Under the Moors, Lisbon became a thriving outpost of the peninsula's new management. Alfama is the city's oldest and most charming

HISTORICAL LANDMARKS

c1200 BC	Phoenicians found a new trading post.
c600 BC	Carthaginians take over the settlement.
205 BC	Absorption into the Roman Empire.
AD 406	First of a succession of Barbarian invasions.
6th century	Visigoths bring a period of stability.
AD 714	Moors conquer city and most of Iberian peninsula.
1147	Lisbon taken from the Moors by Afonso Henriques.
c1260	Lisbon becomes capital of reconquered Portugal.
1386	Alliance with England.
1387	Marriage of João I and Philippa of Lancaster.
15th century	The start of Portugal's golden age; Henry the Navigator founds his 'school of navigation'; foreign exploration leads to the establishment of colonies.
c1500	Expulsion of Jews.
c1550	Inquisition.
1580	Philip II of Spain claims the Portuguese throne; Union of the two crowns.
1640	Portuguese independence restored.
1755	Earthquake, fire and tidal wave devastate Lisbon.
1807	French troops occupy Lisbon; the Portuguese royal family flee to Brazil.
1809-11	British and Portuguese armies under Wellesley expel the French.
1908	Assassination of Carlos I.
1910	Republican rising; Manuel II flees the country.
1916	Portugal joins the Allies in World War I.
1932	Dr Salazar becomes Prime Minister.
1968	Salazar incapacitated and Dr Caetano takes over.
1974	The 'red carnation' revolution; the government is overthrown by the Movement of the Armed Forces.
1975	Democratic elections. Left-wing revolt fails.
1986	Portugal joins the European Union (formerly European Community) and receives EU grants.

residential area and retains its original Arabic name, along with twisting narrow streets.

Although the Christians had kept a precarious foothold in northern Portugal, it was not until 1128 that their struggle began to succeed, when Dom Afonso Henriques became the first king of Portugal. He consolidated his position by defeating the Moslems at the Battle of Ourique in 1139. Lisbon, however, eluded his grasp for another eight years, for the Moors were too securely ensconced in what is now the Castle of St George.

In 1147 the king recruited a volunteer force of thousands of Flemish, Norman, German and English crusaders who

---

Made in Portugal

Although the Portuguese are known for their wonderful *azulejo* designs, the most spectacular home-grown trademark is in the style of architecture and stonecarving which suddenly appeared in Portugal in the 1490s. It flourished for only a few decades, more or less matching the reign of Manuel I (1495-1521), and was later given the name 'Manueline'.

Probably triggered by the great ocean voyages of discovery, it took late Gothic as a base and added fanciful and dramatic decoration, especially references to the sea. Stone was carved like knotted rope and it was sculpted into imitation coral, seahorses, nets and waves as well as nonnautical designs.

The style first appeared in the Igreja de Jesus in Setúbal (see p.68), the Torre de Belém (see p.44), and in the Mosteiro dos Jerónimos (see p.41). It reached a peak of complexity in the unfinished chapels at Batalha (see p.76). In the 16th century the style became less popular and by 1540 Portugal had joined the rest of Europe, building in the Renaissance image.

were passing through on their way to the Holy Land. He convinced the crusaders to stay long enough to strike a blow against the Moslems and, perhaps no less gratifying, to collect the booty of Lisbon.

The Portuguese and the crusaders joined forces and besieged Lisbon for four months. As the Moorish survivors fled, the victors surged in to grab the loot that was left behind. A century later the reconquest of Portugal was completed, and King Afonso III (1248-79) chose Lisbon as his capital.

Golden Age

A decisive battle was fought in 1385 at Aljubarrota, about 100km (60 miles) north of Lisbon. João of Avis, recently proclaimed King João I of Portugal, secured independence from Spain by defeating the army of Juan I of Castile, with the help of English archers. A new alliance with England was sealed in the 1386 Treaty of Windsor, calling for true and eternal friendship. A year later João of Avis married Philippa of Lancaster, the daughter of John of Gaunt. Their third surviving son, the Duke of Viseu, Master of the Order of Christ, changed the map of the world. He is better known as Henry the Navigator.

Prince Henry won his spurs at the age of 21 when

The rocky heights above Sintra are crowned by the ramparts of an old Moorish castle.

he sailed from Lisbon with a daring expedition which captured the Moorish stronghold of Ceuta in 1415. It was his first and last act of derring-do, for he retired then to the 'end-of-the-world', the Sagres peninsula in the Algarve, where he established a school of navigation in which he gathered astronomers, cartographers and other scientists who multiplied the skills of mariners. With single-minded determination, he set up expeditions that pushed back the horizon, and during his lifetime Portuguese caravels sailed far beyond the westernmost point of Africa. With the colonization of Madeira and the Azores, the foundations of the future Portuguese empire were being swiftly laid.

The king who ruled over Portugal's golden age of exploration – and exploitation – was Manuel I (1495-1521). Discoveries made during his reign assured his position as one of Europe's richest rulers and he could well afford monuments as elegant as the Tower of Belém and as impressive as the Jerónimos Monastery. The style of building which eased Portugal from the Gothic into the Renaissance still bears his name: Manueline architecture is whimsically flamboyant and decorative, especially with references to the sea.

One of the capital's most fascinating museums is the ever-colourful Azulejo Museum.

The most significant expedition under Manuel's flag was Vasco da Gama's sea voyage from Lisbon in the summer of 1497. Rounding what is now known as the Cape of Good Hope, he found what Columbus had been looking for in the wrong direction – the sea-route to the spices of the East – thus ending the Venetian monopoly on Eastern trade and attracting merchants from all over Europe to Lisbon. Further territories were discovered – albeit accidentally – in 1500, when the Portuguese explorer Pedro Álvares Cabral unwittingly reached Brazil.

Times of Trial

When Manuel died in 1521, he was succeeded by his son, João the Pious. With one eye on the ungodly ways of prosperous Lisbon and the other on the Inquisition in Spain, João invited the Jesuits to cross the border into Portugal and, in an effort to preserve both academic and moral standards, moved Lisbon's university to Coimbra, where it remains to this day (other universities have since been established in the capital).

Although the Inquisition never really attained major proportions in Portugal, many Jews, including some who had fled from Spain, were forced either to embrace Christianity or face expulsion. Even then, the 'New Christians', as the converts were called, were the subject of repeated investigations by the inquisitors and some were burned at the stake. Regardless of the witchhunts, earthquakes and an outbreak of plague, however, by the end of the century Lisbon had attracted so many people from outlying areas that its population was estimated at 100,000.

Hard times were to follow, though, for the population of the nation in general was sorely depleted, many having left for the new colonies. When the king (and cardinal) Dom Henrique died leaving no heir in 1580, King Philip II of Spain marched in and forced the union of the two crowns.

It took 60 years for the local forces to organize a successful uprising against the occupation. On 1 December 1640 – a date which is still celebrated as Portugal's Restoration Day – Spanish rule was finally overthrown and the Duke of Bragança was crowned King João IV in a joyful ceremony in Lisbon's huge riverfront square, the Terreiro do Paço (now the Praça do Comércio).

His grandson, João V, enjoyed a long and glittering reign (1706-50). As money poured in from gold discoveries in Brazil, the king spent it on lavish monuments and buildings (including the aqueduct which still brings fresh water into the centre of Lisbon.) His best-known extravagance was the palace and monastery at Mafra, 40km (25 miles) north west of the capital. In another effort to enhance the grandeur of his court and country, the king convinced the pope to promote the see of Lisbon to a patriarchate. Meanwhile little

---

A Poet's Saga

Like his Spanish contemporary, Cervantes, Portugal's greatest literary figure had first-hand experience of prison and war.

Luís Vaz de Camões (c.1524-80) – Camoens in English – lost his right eye in a battle for the North African outpost of Ceuta, where he served for two years. Returning to Lisbon in 1550, he was sent to prison in 1553 for taking part in a street fracas, and was only released on his volunteering to travel to India. He later spent years in the Far East, notably Macau, and Mozambique. Shipwrecked in the Mekong Delta off Indochina in 1558, he swam to safety with one arm; with the other, he held aloft the manuscript of his most imperishable work, Os Lusíadas (The Lusiads). This Homeric-style epic, tells the saga of the Portuguese explorers and also recalls in one episode the murder of Inês de Castro (see p.76).

After Camões died, in near poverty, his fame multiplied and so did his poetry. Posthumous sonnets – apocryphal or outright forgeries – tripled the number of his published works.

---

was done to help the ordinary people of Portugal, who were overburdened with taxes to fund the king's extravagance.

Destruction and Rebuilding

The great divide between early history and modern times in Portugal falls around the middle of the 18th century. On All Saints' Day, 1 November 1755, as the crowds packed the churches to honour the dead, Lisbon was devastated by one of the worst earthquakes ever recorded. Churches crumbled, the waters of the Tagus heaved into a tidal wave, while fires spread throughout the city. The triple disaster is estimated to have killed between 15,000 and 60,000 people. Reminders of the nightmare are found in many parts of Lisbon to this day. The most dramatic is the shell of the Carmelite church on a hill above the city's main square, which has been open to the sky ever since the morning the roof fell in.

Routine problems of state were beyond the talents of the ineffectual King José I (1750-77), who could not be expected to cope with the challenge of post-quake recovery. So it was that the task of rebuilding fell to the power behind the throne, a tough, ambitious and tyrannical minister known as Sebastião José de Carvalho e Melo, who later became the Count of Oeiras and is best remembered as the Marquês de Pombal. Taking advantage of the power vacuum, once the earth had stopped shaking, he mobilized all of Portugal's resources for the clean-up. The survivors were fed and housed, the corpses disposed of, the ruins cleared, and then an ambitious project for a new structured city was laid out. Today the modern sections of the capital are aptly referred to as Pombaline Lisbon.

Pombal's achievements are commemorated with his heroic statue on top of a column at the north end of the Avenida da Liberdade. The choked traffic circle is usually referred to as

'Pombal'. The huge equestrian statue of King José holds the main place of honour in the Praça do Comércio, where it was fawningly erected during his lifetime. The king had a close brush with death in an assassination attempt in 1758, after which Pombal inaugurated a reign of terror, complete with public executions and widespread repression. José finally died of natural causes in 1777. The very next day, Pombal was out of a job and banished to his estates.

The Peninsular War

At the beginning of the 19th century, Napoleon managed to drag Portugal into the heat of Europe's conflicts. The situation became so perilous at one time that the royal family fled to Brazil, courtesy of the English boats at their disposal to reach Rio de Janeiro. They were taking no chances and remained there until 1821, ten years after the crisis was over.

When France increased the pressure on Portugal to abandon its traditional loyalty to England, Lisbon tried to stay

The 13th-century cloisters of Lisbon's cathedral still show the effects of the 1755 earthquake.

neutral. In 1807, Napoleon demanded that Portugal do the impossible – declare war on Britain. Responding to the predictable veto, the French army under Junot marched in, setting up his headquarters in the pink palace at Queluz. For months the people of Lisbon had to live with the sight of Napoleon's colours flying high over the Castelo de São Jorge.

Military miscalculations in the face of a British expedition sent Junot's army packing in 1808. Throughout the next few years repeat engagements became notable victories for the combined Portuguese-British forces, who owed much to the strategic brilliance of the great British commander, Sir Arthur Wellesley (later known as the Duke of Wellington). After the textbook battle of the Lines of Torres Vedras, north of Lisbon, the French began a long retreat, sacking and looting as they passed. Napoleon's last outpost in Portugal was evacuated in the spring of 1811.

Civil War

Peace was still to prove elusive, though, and only 22 years later the country was again at war – this time in its most tragic variety, brother against brother. Pedro IV, previously emperor of Brazil (which had asserted its independence from Portugal), fought to wrest the crown from Miguel I, his absolutist brother. Pedro won, but he died of consumption only a few months later. He was just 36 years old. His adolescent daughter, Maria da Glória, assumed the throne. She married the German nobleman, Ferdinand of Saxe-Coburg-Gotha, who built her the astonishing Pena Palace above Sintra and fathered her five sons and six daughters. Maria II died in childbirth at the age of 34.

Premature and tragic deaths claimed many Portuguese royals, but in all the country's history only one king was ever assassinated. The victim was Carlos I, the date 1 February

1908. Like many other crucial events, it occurred in Lisbon's vast Terreiro do Paço, now more commonly called the Praga do Comércio. As the royal family was riding past in an open carriage, an assassin's bullet caught Carlos in the head. A few seconds later another conspirator fatally shot Carlos' son and heir, Prince Luís Felipe. A third bullet hit the young prince Manuel in the arm. Thus wounded and haunted, Manuel II began a brief 2-year reign as Portugal's last king. He was deposed on 5 October 1910 in a republican uprising supported by certain elements of the armed forces. The royal yacht took him to Gibraltar and later England, where he lived in exile.

Into Modern Europe

The republican form of government was as unstable as it was unfamiliar. Resignations, coups and assassinations kept an unhappy merry-go-round of presidents and prime ministers whirling. The nation could ill afford a war; nonetheless, German threats to its African territories – among other motives – edged Portugal into World War I on the side of the Allies. On 24 February 1916, the Portuguese navy seized a group of German ships anchored in the Tagus and the Kaiser replied with the inevitable declaration of war. A Portuguese expeditionary force sailed for the trenches of France.

The war's toll hastened the end of Portugal's unsuccessful attempt at democracy. After a revolution in 1926, General António Óscar Carmona took over as strongman. Two years later he entrusted the economy to António de Oliveira Salazar, an austere economics professor at Coimbra University. The exhausted Portuguese finances immediately perked up.

In 1932 Dr Salazar became Prime Minister. His tough authoritarian regime – the *Estado Novo* (New State) – was in favour of economic progress and nationalism. He kept Portugal neutral in World War II, but permitted the Allies to use

Where great voyages of discovery began,
Lisbon's waterfront welcomes the world's trade.

the Azores. Unlike his fellow-dictator, Franco of Spain, Dr Salazar avoided a personality cult; his portrait never graced the stamps of his realm.

When a massive stroke felled Salazar in 1968, the reins were handed to a former rector of the University of Lisbon, Dr Marcelo Caetano. In 1974 the armed forces, discontent with fighting the hopeless colonial wars, overthrew the dictatorship in the 'red carnation' revolution. Portugal disengaged from its seething African possessions and absorbed the million or so refugees who fled to a motherland most had never seen. The nation suffered several years of political confusion before learning to live in a democracy. With its entry into the European Union (formerly the European Community) in 1986, the pace of development suddenly quickened. Although the economic climate of the 1990s has become somewhat harsher, Portugal still looks to the future with confidence.

WHERE TO GO

Lisbon's waterfront is an arc stretching for nearly 32km (20 miles) along the River Tagus (*Tejo* in Portuguese). Many of the greatest sights in this city are within walking distance of the river, but because of the hills and the way in which the sights are spread out, it is not always very easy to go directly from one to the other.

You can travel cheaply and efficiently from place to place by public transport. Buses are quick and it's not very difficult to learn the system. Antique trams ply some routes, and funiculars climb steep hills. Lisbon's Metro – the underground railway or subway – is modern and fast, but serves only a limited area. Taxis are usually plentiful and fairly inexpensive. Although traffic jams in Lisbon are growing, they are still not as fierce as in some bigger capitals; nonetheless, rush hour – about 7.30-10am and 5-7pm – is best avoided, on both the roads and, for an hour or so at least, the Metro as well. Parking is difficult or impossible on weekdays, so a car is really only useful for out-of-town excursions.

> **Underground fare in Lisbon is the same irrespective of the distance you travel.**

On arrival a guided city tour can be a good way to grasp the general layout (see p.115).

THE CENTRE

Praça do Comércio (Commerce Square) is one of few extravagant touches in this city of modest people and places. Stately pink arcades line all three sides of the vast plaza; the fourth is open to the harbour, with Venetian-style stairs leading down to the edge of the water.

Before the 1755 earthquake had wiped out all the buildings around the plaza, it was called the Terreiro do Paço (Palace Square) – the name by which it is still informally known – after the Ribeira Palace, which stood here until that time. The less haphazard post-quake layout is more harmonious, but today the square is so overrun with traffic that the regal effect is somewhat diminished.

The bronze **statue** of a man in a plumed helmet on horseback represents King José I, patron of Lisbon's great city-planner, the Marquês de Pombal, who designed the square (see p.19). Another sculptural flourish is the triumphal arch connecting government buildings on the north of the square.

Through this arch you can travel the length of Rua Augusta, the main street of this rigidly rectangular 18th-century part of town. Critics find all the identically sized buildings monotonous, though the severity is relieved by original decorative touches such as tiled façades with different designs and colours. After the disaster of 1755, all buildings on these 15 side streets were constructed to be earthquake-proof. The area is called the **Baixa**, and is full of shops, banks, tea-shops and small restaurants.

The top end of Rua Augusta runs into the **Rossio**, Lisbon's main square. In

The Rossio's violent history has given way to a more peaceful – but no less colourful – present.

LISBON HIGHLIGHTS

For anyone in a hurry, the list below pinpoints Lisbon's main sights. Opening times are also given (where applicable), along with directions and public transport details.

Castelo de São Jorge: the old citadel of the Moors commands impressive views of the city from its ramparts. The castle has been restored and has pleasant gardens within its walls, which are home to a variety of tame birds, including peacocks and pelicans. Open daily 9am-7pm (later in summer); free. Bus 37 from Praça da Figueira. (See p.30)

Cathedral (Sé): this fortress-like church was begun in the 12th century and now boasts fine tombs. Open Mon-Sat 9am-noon, 2-5pm; there is a small fee for entrance to the cloisters and museum of treasures. Tram 28, or a short walk from Praça do Comércio. (See p.33)

Igreja de Santo Estêvão and the **Alfama district**: a fine 13th-century church in the midst of the oldest part of Lisbon – a labyrinth of stone stairs and alleyways, white-washed houses and red-tiled roofs which follow the Moorish pattern. Tram 28 or bus 37 and walk down. (See p.36)

Igreja do Carmo: this magnificent Gothic church, completed in 1423, has been open to the skies ever since it was ruined in the 1755 earthquake. Also here is a collection of tiles and other relics (small fee). Open Mon-Sat 9.30am-5pm (6pm in summer); free. Near top of Elevador de Santa Justa. (See p.39)

Mosteiro dos Jerónimos: Belém's massive monastery, dating from the early 16th century, is adorned with all manner of architectural embellishments. Open Tue-Sun 10am-noon, 2-5pm (6.30pm in summer); fee for the Manueline cloisters. Bus 43 from Praça da Figuera or tram 15 from Praça do Comércio. (See p.41)

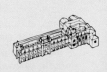

Torre de Belém: a famous, decorative 16th-century tower, regarded as the epitome of Portugal's Manueline architecture. Open Tue-Sat 10am-1pm, 2.30-5pm (6.30pm in summer); entry fee. Bus 43 from Praça da Figuera or tram 15 from Praça do Comércio. (See p.44)

Ponte 25 de Abril: a soaring suspension bridge over the River Tagus, built 1962-66 and renamed in 1974 to commemorate the revolution. Toll for the bridge. Details of buses at the tourist office. (See p.45)

Statue of Christ the King: modelled on Rio de Janeiro's statue, this 100m (330ft) landmark was erected in 1959 in gratitude to Dr Salazar for keeping Portugal out of World War II. Superb views across the Tagus to Lisbon. Take the ferry from Praça do Comércio to Cacilhas, then bus or taxi. (See p.46)

Aguas Livres Aqueduct: this architectural showpiece, completed in 1748, withstood the earthquake of 1755. The aqueduct is 18km (11 miles) long in total and still carries water to the city. Its 14 arches lie in the Amoreiras district; there are good views from Monsanto Park. Bus 15 or tram 24, 26. (See p.47)

days gone by this was the shocking scene of public hangings, bullfights and witch-burning. Today, it is still the main centre of activity in Lisbon – the place to window-shop, meet friends, drink coffee, watch the busy crowds go by from sidewalk cafés, and listen to the fountains and the incomprehensible calls of the newsboys and flower sellers. The Rossio is also the most popular place to queue for a taxi or bus.

The statue on the column in the square honours Pedro IV (1826-34), who was the first emperor of Brazil. A persistent legend maintains that it is not Pedro at all, but a discarded statue of his doomed contemporary, Emperor Maximilian of Mexico, which turned up cheap at a surplus sale. Official sources deny this story.

The Rossio suburban railway station looks at first like a vision of a Moorish palace. Actually, it's a romantic effort of the late 19th century in the style now formally known as neo-Manueline.

Exotic arches distinguish the Rossio station façade.

Confusingly, the Rossio sits side by side with yet another major square, known as the Praça da Figueira. This square is built around an equestrian statue of King João I, founder of the Avis dynasty. It's usually plastered with hungry pigeons all waiting to be fed.

Back to the Rossio and past the Teatro Nacional (National Theatre), a fairly straightforward obelisk marks the Praça dos Restauradores, which celebrates the overthrow of Spanish rule in 1640. Palácio Foz, the once splendid palace situated on the west side of the square, houses a **tourist information office**. A nearby funicular climbs to the top of the Bairro Alto (see p.37).

From here the Avenida da Liberdade makes its way uphill for a little over 1km (0.6 mile). Among statues, fountains, ponds and flower gardens are benches on which to pause for a while and contemplate your surroundings. The boulevard ends at the traffic circle called Praça Marquês de Pombal (or Rotunda), from which an elevated statue of the dictator (inexplicably accompanied by a lion) looks out over his works.

> **Post offices are indicated by the letters CTT (***Correios e Telecomunicações***).**

In an effective reflection of the boulevard, the formal park – **Parque Eduardo VII** – continues uphill beyond Pombal. The well-manicured lawns and shrubs seem to be a northward extension of the avenue. On either side are wooded areas and gardens. So thrilled were the Portuguese by a royal visit at the turn of the century that they named the park after England's Kind Edward VII.

Lisbon's most original botanical triumph occupies the north-west corner of this park. Known as **Estufa Fria** ('cold greenhouse'), it is a tropical rainforest right in the heart of a European capital. Plants and flowers from Africa, Asia and

South America feel completely at home here in the Lisbon air, all thanks to a simple system of slatted roofs and walls which filters the extremes of weather.

A more recent addition, a huge standard greenhouse, accommodates the more delicate plants and trees, and the whole enterprise is surrounded on the outside by marvellous displays of Lisbon's indigenous flora.

OLD LISBON

Almost every hill in town has a *miradouro* (belvedere), but the best panorama of all belongs to the **Castelo de São Jorge** (St George's Castle), which is reached by the steep alley and steps that continue east from Rua de Santa Justa. From the ramparts, you look out across the Baixa to the Bairro Alto (see p.37), down to the river and the Ponte 25 de

The park named after Edward VII of England brings shade and countryside to the heart of Lisbon.

Abril (see p.45), along as far as Belém (see p.40), and across to the hills beyond the south bank.

The Moslems who ruled Portugal between the 8th and 12th centuries dug in well but were finally dislodged in 1147. The new proprietor – Dom Afonso Henriques – succeeded in expanding the fortifications, but earthquakes as well as general wear and tear over the following centuries left little intact. Restoration since, however, has given new life to the old ruins.

Aside from the sensational vistas and the chance to roam the battlements, the castle is worth a visit for the park inside its walls. Platoons of birds strut around as if they own the place – not just transient pigeons and sparrows, but resident peacocks, pheasants, pelicans, flamingos, swans, geese and ducks. As black and white are Lisbon's colours, you will see black ravens and albino birds – all watched over with affection by the municipality.

Since literally dozens of Lisbon churches are of historic or artistic merit, the ones included here are those of most significance. **São Vicente de Fora** (St Vincent Beyond the Walls) is noticeable due to its twin towers rising above a hillside east of the castle. Reconstructed in the 16th century around the time of the Inquisition, this building is huge by local standards, yet it succeeds in combining mass and grace.

It's all very Italianate, from the statues of saints in their niches on the façade to the grand baroque altar. The architect was an Italian, Filippo Terzi, who is said to have been inspired by the Jesuit church in Rome. St Vincent's interior – a single nave and vaulted ceiling – has clean, crisp lines like a technical drawing from a design manual.

On the right, as you face the altar, a heavy wooden door leads to the monastic cloister – and a surprise. The walls are lined with *azulejos*, blue-and-white glazed tiles, depicting scenes of 18th-century French life and leisure, along with the animal *Fables* of La Fontaine. The pantheon just near to the cloister contains tombs of the Bragança kings and queens, from the first of the dynasty, João IV, to the last, Manuel II. Even Catherine of Bragança, queen of Charles II of England, is buried here. She returned to Lisbon after he died.

Behind the church, in the Campo de Santa Clara, a **market** (known as *Feira da Ladra* or Thieves' Market) is held on Tuesday and Saturday. On the fringes of the kitchenware and workaday clothing stalls, antique collectors may uncover a valuable old clock, or at least a rusty iron. The range of second-hand items is incredible.

The severe Renaissance lines of São Vicente de Fora contrast with the twisting alleys of Alfama.

Directly downhill, the grandiose marble church with a high dome reminiscent of the Capitol building in Washington is the **Pantheon of Santa Engrácia**. Construction began in the 17th century, but the cupola wasn't completed until 1966. Thus it is that in Lisbon today, the description of something as the 'works of Santa Engrácia' is synonomous with saying it is an endless task.

Santa Engrácia was actually a church until a few years ago, when it was deconsecrated and became a

Saints of Lisbon

Lisbon's favourite saint is known elsewhere as St Anthony of Padua. In Lisbon, however, he is called St Anthony (Santo António) of Lisbon, for it was here that he was born, a few doors down from the cathedral, in 1195. According to legend, when his words went unheard by man, he preached to the fish, and so became patron saint of the lower animals after being posthumously canonized by Gregory IX in 1232. Preacher, theologian, patron of the poor, and defender of human rights, he died in Padua in Italy in 1231. Today he is often depicted accompanied by an ass.

The official patron saint of Lisbon is St Vincent (São Vicente), a 4th-century martyr. The first king of Portugal, Dom Afonso Henriques, ordered his remains to be shipped from the Algarve to Lisbon. Two ravens faithfully escorted the saintly relics, which explains why many a Lisbon lamppost bears the symbol of a sailing ship with a bird fore and aft.

'Pantheon', not dedicated to the gods as in ancient Rome, but to the greatest men in Portuguese history, those who are honoured with symbolic tombs in the sumptuous rotunda. To one side are the real tombs of presidents of the republic. You can sometimes climb to the base of the dome for a view down onto the marble floor of the rotunda. Outside a terrace overlooks the rooftops.

Some old cities are built round their cathedrals, set facing a square of civic buildings. This is not the case with Lisbon. Without so much as a modest plaza to set it off, the city's **cathedral** (*Sé*) appears out of nowhere at a bend in the road (most easily reached from the centre by continuing east on the extension of Rua da Conceção). Don't misinterpret its reticence, for this is a handsome cathedral with great historic and artistic importance.

Begun as a fortress-church in the 12th century, its towers and walls, still with firing slits, suggest a beleaguered citadel. The church was damaged by earthquakes during the 14th, 16th and 18th centuries, so architectural touches now range from Romanesque and Gothic to baroque. One relic of the 18th century, the organ, still has a robust voice.

In a chapel off the apse at the eastern end you can see a couple of sentimental 14th-century **tombs**. The statue of a bearded man, Lopo Fernandes Pacheco, lies on his sarcophagus with his hand on a sword and his favourite dog at his feet; on an adjacent stone coffin, a statue of his second wife reads her prayer book, accompanied by three dogs, two of them fighting.

For more medieval memories, ask to be admitted to the 13th-century **cloister**. There, amidst the signs of earthquake damage, you can see parts of pre-Roman and Roman statues, columns and inscriptions. One old chapel has a brilliantly wrought-iron screen complete with intricate Moorish and Romanesque designs.

A few steps down the hill, the church of Santo António da Sé, built in 1812, honours Lisbon's revered native son, St Anthony of Padua. The crypt of this church was built on the spot where, according to local lore, his house stood. Among various roles, St Anthony is the patron saint of women looking for husbands, and sometimes bridal bouquets are left at his altar in the cathedral, along with thanks for all his good work.

Between here and the waterfront, at Campo das Cebolas, the **Casa dos Bicos** (House of Facets) is worth a glance. Built during the early 16th century, it belonged to the illegitimate son of Afonso de Albuquerque, the Viceroy of Portuguese India. The building is faced with pyramid-shaped stones.

The Rua dos Bacalhoeiros (Street of the Cod-Sellers), on which the house stands, is now lined with small shops. One sells corks for flasks and bottles of all shapes and sizes, another is piled high with empty burlap sacks, while yet another stocks nothing but cans of Portuguese sardines and tuna – with or without openers. The west end of the street runs on straight back into the busy waterfront square, the Praça do Comércio.

ALFAMA

Most visitors tend to agree that Alfama is Lisbon's most fascinating area. Here, in the labyrinth of crooked streets, alleys and rickety stairways that go nowhere, you'll get the feeling that nothing has changed since the early Middle Ages. The whole area is a chaos of tilting houses with mismatched windows, bars and fish stalls, as well as laundry dripping onto the street.

You will get lost. Even a map and compass won't help. The Alfama district is a cartographer's nightmare, with its twisting roads going over and under each other and ending at blank walls. You would need a mountain goat's sense of direction to keep on track.

The only solution is to follow your nose and learn by trial and error. When in

Life goes on at many levels in the narrow streets of Lisbon's Alfama district.

Alfama Highlights

Here are a few of the Alfama area's highlights, some of which you'll probably stumble across by accident, through an arch or round a blind corner. If not, come back another day for more of the area's intriguing sights, sounds and smells.

Rua de São João da Praça: this is where Portugal's first king, Dom Afonso Henriques, entered Lisbon through the Moorish wall on 25 October 1147.

Igreja de São Miguel (St Michael's Church): built in the 12th century, restored during the 18th, with a glorious ceiling of Brazilian jacaranda wood. It's dark inside, but the caretaker turns on the lights so you can see the rococo gilt altar screen.

Beco da Cardosa: an alley with blind-alley offshoots, the very essence of Alfama's higgledy-piggledy appeal.

Igreja de Santo Estêvão (St Stephen's Church): with a 13th-century, octagonal floor-plan, but rebuilt several times over the years. The overhanging back of the church nearly collides with the front gate of an old palace.

Beco do Carneiro (Sheep Alley): ancient houses sag towards each other across a step-street barely wide enough for two people. Look up: it's not a trick of perspective, the eaves of the buildings really do touch.

Rua de São Pedro: Alfama's boisterous main shopping street, too narrow for cars. Fruit and vegetables are cheaper than downtown; fishwives shriek amidst a cacophony of chickens, dogs and children.

Largo de São Rafael: remains of a tower, part of the Moorish defences which were finally overwhelmed in 1147.

doubt, stick to the narrow streets. If you find yourself in a conventional street wide enough for both a car and a pedestrian, then you have strayed from the Alfama area.

You could start at the southern extremities of the neighbourhood – Largo do Chafariz de Dentro or Largo do Terreiro do Trigo. It's much easier, though, to begin at the top, at Largo do Salvador or Largo das Portas do Sol, and let gravity lead you back down towards the river.

For a stunning view over the city, pause at the **Miradouro de Santa Luzia** on the edge of Alfama, just below Portas do Sol. From the tiled balcony perched on a bluff you look straight down onto a charming jumble of tiled roofs. Meanwhile, in the little park here, old men in black berets take the sun, play cards and survey the tourists with typical good-natured curiosity.

Look for the two remarkably detailed and dramatic *azulejos* (tile panels) on the wall facing the belvedere. One of them shows Lisbon's waterfront as it was before the great earthquake, while the other depicts with bloodthirsty detail the rout of the Moors from the Castelo de São Jorge (Castle of St George) in 1147.

Wander at will and don't worry if you haven't got a clue where you're going; just keep heading downhill and eventually you will come out at the River Tagus.

BAIRRO ALTO

Like the steep Alfama area, the Bairro Alto ('high neighbourhood') is a hilly section full of evocative old houses, their wrought-iron balconies hung with birdcages and flowerpots. At night the local *fado* nightclubs are loaded with atmosphere and attract visitors from afar. This is Lisbon's bohemian district, popular with local revellers who party from one disco or bar to another. Some venues are well hid-

Hop on the Elevador da Gloria funicular and climb the steep slope to the Bairro Alto from Praça dos Restauradores.

den behind anonymous doors or guarded by huge bouncers who only admit those they like the look of; others, such as a few seedy strip shows, are all too eager to take your money. There is no need to worry, though; this area is busy enough at night to be safe, not least thanks to the many restaurants. During the day it is slightly calmer and quieter, but still intriguing to wander around.

Whatever your pleasure, the easiest way to reach the Bairro Alto is to board the eccentric yellow **funicular** trolley at Praça dos Restauradores. The hill is walkable, but for the cost of a bus ticket the funicular is far more fun, and just a little romantic.

At the top end of the brief journey, the city council has built a lookout park called the Miradouro de São Pedro de Alcântara. Though you can see no more than a slice of the river, the **panorama** includes a good view of the Castelo de São Jorge head-on across the valley. A tile orientation table, slightly out of date, helps you identify the landmarks.

Next to the *miradouro* lies the **Jardim Botânico** (Botanical Garden), reached through the university gate alongside the Academy of Sciences. It likes to concentrate on the scientific cultivation of unusual plants from distant climes, but this serious activity doesn't disturb the lush beauty and overall tranquillity. The tree-shaded gardens slope steeply downhill to a lower gate near the Avenida Metro station.

Two churches in the upper town are unusual enough to rate your attention. Just down the street from the top of the funicular, the **Igreja de São Roque** has a dull exterior – the original 16th-century façade perished in the 1755 earthquake – but inside you will see some of the most lavishly decorated chapels in Lisbon. The baroque **altar** of the chapel of São João Baptista (St John the Baptist), on the left, is a wealth of gold, silver, bronze, agate, amethyst, lapis lazuli, ivory and Carrara marble. In 1742 King João V of Portugal sent orders to Rome, where teams of artists and artisans worked on this altar for five whole years. Then the pope gave his blessing and the altar was dismantled and shipped to the customer, an incredible prefabricated masterpiece.

Alongside the church, the Museu de Arte Sacra (Museum of Sacred Art) contains a collection of precious reliquaries, delicately worked jewellery and vestments.

Heading downhill, the **Igreja do Carmo** (the Carmelite Church) is rich only in memories, dating back to the 14th century, when it was built. As you stand on the grass inside the shell of what was once one of Lisbon's greatest churches, look up through the rebuilt arches into the blue sky and imagine the scene that day in 1755 when the roof fell in on a full congregation.

Quite a modest archaeological museum has been established inside the part of the church which is still roofed; it is a hodgepodge of prehistoric pottery, Roman sculptures, a few early Portuguese tombs, and even a few ancient mummies under glass.

The fastest way to reach the centre of town from here is by the **Elevador de Santa Justa** (built by Raúl Mesnier, and not by Gustave Eiffel as most reports claim), a vertical variation of the funiculars used elsewhere in town. This lift, inaugurated in 1902, was originally powered by steam. Rebuilt in 1993, it is 30m (100ft) high and quite a remarkable sight in itself.

The longer and slower way downhill weaves through the **Chiado** district, whose zigzagging streets have for centuries been renowned for Lisbon's most elegant goods – silverware, leather, fashions, books – and fine pastry and tea shops. In 1988, however, the area was devastated by fire, resulting in two of Europe's oldest department stores being wiped out. Reconstruction is under way and makes quite a spectacle, with up to six storeys below street level as well as four or five above.

West of the Bairro Alto lies a truly delightful park officially called Jardim Guerra Junqueiro, and unofficially known as **Estrela** (star), the name of the distinguished 18th-century church across the street. Abundant tropical foliage plus the customary ducks, geese, peacocks and peasants – and a belvedere offering yet another angle on the city and its harbour – are all here.

BELÉM

As the seagull flies, Belém (Portuguese for Bethlehem) lies about 6km (4 miles) west of Praça do Comércio. This Lisbon district has more than its share of grand monuments and museums. Land has been reclaimed from the river here to provide parkland and marinas, so the shore itself is unrecognizable; but this is where the great Portuguese voyages of discovery in the 15th and 16th centuries actually began.

Start a visit to Belém at the edge closest to central Lisbon. The **Museu Nacional dos Coches** (National Coach Museum) is housed, aptly, in the former riding school of the Belém Royal Palace. Two grand halls display dozens of impressive carriages which have been drawn by the royal horses for ceremonial occasions both in the city and cross-country over four centuries. The most extravagant are three sculpted, gilt carriages used by the Portuguese embassy in Rome in the early 18th century to impress Pope Clement XI.

One coach after another illustrates the painfully slow evolution of technical details leading up to the sleek 19th-century Crown Carriage, still worthy of any royal procession. Even the various riding accessories used by royalty, ranging from stirrups to coachhorns, are on show.

Only a short stroll westward along the Rua de Belém, you will arrive at Lisbon's biggest and most admirable religious monument, the **Mosteiro dos Jerónimos** (Jerónimos Monastery). This monastery was begun by Manuel I with all the riches brought back by Portuguese ships from the East. The convent wing was, unfortunately, destroyed in the 1755 earthquake, but the church and cloister survive, testaments to 16th-century faith and style.

The vast south façade of the church, parallel to the river, is mostly unadorned limestone, and the few embellishments

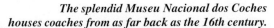

The splendid Museu Nacional dos Coches houses coaches from as far back as the 16th century.

that have been included – such as the stone 'rope' – really sing out. The main portal is a wonder of intricate stonework. Inside the church, tall columns carved in typical designs of the Manueline era (which bridged the gap between Gothic and Renaissance styles in Portugal) contribute to a feeling of infinite height and space. The first architect in charge was a Frenchman called Diogo Boytac, who was succeeded by the Spaniard João de Castilho.

Although it's usually quite dark inside the church, you should be able to pick out several royal tombs, set on pompous sculptured elephants in a bizarre tribute to the new discovered marvels of the East.

Near the west door are the modern tombs of two other giants of Portugal's golden age, Vasco da Gama and the poet Luís de Camões.

Once you leave the church (don't miss the fine sculptural work surrounding the exterior of the west portal), turn right

An early example of the Manueline style,
the 16th-century Mosteiro dos Jerónimos at Belém.

for the cloister, an airy double-decker structure of strikingly original proportions and perspectives. As you stroll round the arcades, the very dimensions of the place seem to change because of the clever intersection of both sharp angles and arches. No two columns are the same.

The west part of the monastery has been largely restored and now houses the **Museu Nacional de Arqueológia** (the National Museum of Archaeology). This is a very important collection of ancient relics – Bronze Age jewels, Stone Age tools, and from Roman days, excellent sculptures as well as mosaics.

The educational attractions continue just to the west with a planetarium, contributed by Portugal's ubiquitous benefactor, Calouste Gulbenkian.

In the west end of the monastery and overflowing into new buildings beyond, the **Museu da Marinha** (Naval Museum) will appeal to anyone interested in history or the sea (see p.49). Countless model ships of all ages, often fiendishly intricate, are displayed here. Perhaps one of the most startling exhibits is the huge galliot or brigantine built in 1785 to celebrate a royal marriage, with seats for 80 oarsmen. Next to it is the seaplane which first flew the South Atlantic.

Close at hand is the **Centro Cultural de Belém**, a modern building designed to house the EU (formely EC) Presidency each time it is hosted by Portugal, with all the accoutrements of an international congress centre which even extends to an opera house.

Between the monastery and the river is a garden with rose beds, swan ponds and bird of paradise flowers. The Fonte Luminosa (luminous fountain) can be hooked up to provide a 45-minute show of changing light and colour patterns.

The modern **Padrão dos Descobrimentos** (Monument to the Discoveries) juts from the riverbank like a caravel cresting a wave. On the prow stands Prince Henry the Navigator,

Trace Portuguese discoveries, the Cape of Good Hope and the route to India, with the help of this map at Belém.

looking out across the river and wearing, as always, his funny round hat. The statues behind him, on both sides of the central shaft, represent noted explorers, astronomers, map-makers, chroniclers and others involved in the dauntless days of discovery. An elevator followed by stairs lead to the top and a superb view.

A compass and map of the world inlaid in the pavement here emphasizes the phenomenal extent of Portugal's exploration during its golden age, from the Azores and Brazil to India, Macau and Japan.

One interesting museum on the waterfront, is the **Museu de Arte Popular** (Popular Art Museum) surveys the folk art and customs of Portugal, region by region, with plenty of charming fabrics, embroidery, furniture, toys and dolls.

Finally, there is the famous **Torre de Belém** (Tower of Belém). It is one of the best examples of Manueline architecture (see p.16) and must have been a wonderful sight for weary explorers returning from their journey. Although it may be familiar from pictures, the tower is probably much smaller than you imagined.

Wander around the waterfront park and watch the sunlight pick out the fine carved details. Then cross the wooden bridge and enter a 16th-century world, where the interior is suddenly austere. The most handsome side is that facing the river, with a lovely loggia.

While you're at this end of town, don't miss the **Palácio da Ajuda**, the biggest palace inside the city limits, which is north of Belém up Calçada da Ajuda, and brims with all kinds of art works and curiosities. Portugal's King Luís I (1861-89) along with his bride Princess Maria Pia of Savoy became the first royal family to live here and were responsible for the lavish furnishings – Gobelin tapestries, oriental ceramics and rare Portuguese furniture, as well as plenty of decorative trinkets of little, or no artistic merit.

Behind a façade resembling a scaled-down Buckingham Palace there are three dining rooms: one for state occasions (seating 50), one upstairs for entertaining 160 close friends, and the intimate but nonetheless lavish family snack spot, which comes with attached billiard room.

Guides point out down-to-earth novelties like the queen's sewing machine in a special rococo case and her bathroom with 'made-in-England' ('tip to empty') wash-basins.

ACROSS THE RIVER TAGUS

The **Ponte 25 de Abril**, across the River Tagus, became the longest suspension bridge in Europe when it was opened to traffic in 1966. It was named in honour of the nation's dictator, but after the revolution of 1974 the word 'Salazar' was removed and for quite a time it was just 'the bridge'. Finally it was renamed after the date of that revolution, 25 April.

You can't stop on it, but the view of Lisbon *from* the bridge is as impressive as the vista from an aeroplane.

Just across the river, above Cacilhas and looming up over the bridge's toll booths, is Lisbon's variation on Rio de Janeiro's landmark, the statue of **Christ the King**. Almost 30m (90ft) tall, it stands on a modern four-pronged pedestal, with a church, the Santuário de Cristo Rei, housed in the base of the monument. Take the lift up to the viewing terrace for a glorious 360-degree **panorama** of the whole River Tagus estuary, the bridge, all Lisbon and a vast expanse of Portugal to the south.

To visit the statue you can drive across the bridge or take one of the **ferryboats** from Praça do Comércio to Cacilhas and then a taxi or a bus marked 'Cristo Rei'. The ferryboat is strongly recommended for its exciting introduction to the port. The commuters may read their newspapers oblivious to the view, but you'll enjoy the ferry's manoeuvrings among ocean liners, tugs, tankers, and freighters. Merchant ships sail from here to the old Portuguese territories – from Rio de Janeiro to Maputo – and wherever else the sea lanes lead.

Coming back from Cacilhas, you can either return to Praça do Comércio or to Cais do Sodré, a few hundred yards west. If possible, head for Cais do Sodré. The railway station here is the place to catch a commuter train for Estoril and Cascais. In this neighbourhood the stores sell buoys, full-size anchors, compasses and engine-room telegraphs – serious maritime equipment, not just for the Sunday sailor. Across the street under an Indian-looking dome is Lisbon's lively main **market**, the Mercado da Ribeira, where more than a thousand people work. Men in padded caps balance unwieldy wicker trays of fruit and vegetables on their heads, and the scent of fresh coriander pervades the air. Since it is both a wholesale and retail market, there is always some-

Salazar Bridge was renamed the Ponte 25 de Abril to commemorate the 1974 revolution.

thing interesting going on, from 2am to 9pm. The best time to absorb the colourful atmosphere is just before lunch, when you can pick up the makings for a great picnic, too.

NORTH LISBON

The biggest landmark in Lisbon keeps popping into your field of vision from the most unexpected places, in and outside of town. That's not at all surprising when you consider it's 18km (11 miles) long. The soaring arches of the **aqueduct** of *Águas Livres* may remind you of ancient Rome, but this is a more recent engineering feat, having been undertaken in the 18th century: the water began pouring into the fountains of central Lisbon in 1748, and still does to this day.

Along with the motorway to Cascais (see p.58), the aqueduct goes through the city's biggest park, **Monsanto**. Eucalyptus, cypress, cedar, umbrella pines and oak trees all thrive on the rolling hillsides. Aside from calm and fresh air the park is well supplied with amenities – sports grounds, bars and restaurants. Its municipal camping ground ranks as one of Europe's prettiest and best organized, and the park also has some impressive *miradouros* (lookout points), giving outstanding views over Lisbon and the estuary. Be warned, though, its roads usually turn into a huge traffic jam at rush hours.

North of the aqueduct is Lisbon's **Jardim Zoológico**, which although set in a lovely park, is an old-style zoo, with little space for the animals to move about. One of the big chimpanzee cages is designed as a wine store with kegs, unbreakable bottles and scales, but the star of the show is a money-spinning elephant who rings a bell and blows a horn when you hand him a coin. Children are well taken care of, with their own little amusement park and a driving school with foot-powered cars. Feeding time is always popular; for the animals it's at 4pm. For everyone else there's a choice of small snack bars, a restaurant, and sidewalk stalls.

Campo Grande, situated between the zoo and the airport, is a popular park with Lisboêtas and visitors alike. Palm, cedar and willow trees shade pretty walks and a small lake with rowing boats.

MUSEUMS

 ### The Gulbenkian Museum

Lisbon's most wondrous museum was created to house the thousands of works of art acquired by the Armenian billionaire, Calouste Gulbenkian. A visit to the pleasant modern gallery will tell you a lot about this great philanthropist, who died in Lisbon in 1955. Clearly he knew what he liked and

MUSEUM HIGHLIGHTS

Museums are usually open Tue-Sun 10am-5pm (some stay open until 6/6.30pm in summer). Most close for lunch 12.30/1pm-2/2.30pm. Entrance charges are usually in the range of 400 esc to 500 esc, but in many cases are waived on Sunday morning or throughout the whole day. The following list gives Lisbon's top museums with suggestions for getting there. Check local listings or ask at a tourist information office for current prices and opening hours (see p.123).

Ancient Art: *Museu Nacional de Arte Antiga, Rua das Janelas Verdes*. Old masters, silver, gold, ceramics, oriental treasures. Bus 27 from Rotunda (Praça Marquês de Pombal) or Belém.

Museu Calouste Gulbenkian, Avenida de Berna at Praça de Espanha. (Closed Wednesday am.) Superb ancient art, ceramics, textiles, sculpture and 15th-20th-century paintings. Metro to São Sebastião; bus 31, 41, 46 from Rossio and Rotunda.

Archaeology: *Museu Nacional de Arqueológia, Mosteiro dos Jerónimos, Praça do Império, Belém*. Discoveries from the Stone Age, Bronze Age, Iron Age and Roman times. Tram 15, 17 from Praça do Comércio; bus 27 from Rotunda.

Azulejos: *Museu do Azulejo, Convento da Madre de Deus*. 16th-18th century tile masterpieces. Bus 59 from Praça Figuera.

Coaches: *Museu dos Coches, Praça Afonso de Albuquerque, Belém*. 16th-19th century royal and other coaches and carriages. Tram 15, 17 from Praça do Comércio; bus 27 from Rotunda.

Decorative Arts: *Museu Escola de Artes Decorativas (Fundacão Ricardo Espirito Santo Silva), Largo das Portas do Sol 2, Alfama*. (Open by appointment only, tel. 886 21 83) Furniture-making, leatherwork, metalwork. Tram 28 from Baixa.

Folk Art: *Museu de Arte Popular, Avenida Brasília, Belém*. Full range of Portuguese folk arts and crafts. Tram 15, 17 from Praça do Comércio; bus 27 from Rotunda.

Military: *Museu Militar (Museu de Artilharia), largo dos Caminhos de Ferro*. Old weapons and armour. Bus 12 from Rotunda.

Naval: *Museu da Marinha, Praça do Império, Belém (housed in Jerónimos Monastery)*. Ship models, royal barges and seaplanes. Tram 15, 17 from Praça do Comércio; bus 27 from Rotunda.

was willing to pay any price to get it. He must have been the terror of all museum directors bidding against him.

This huge collection starts chronologically, with Egyptian ceramics and sculptures going back to about 2700 BC, so delicate and so perfectly preserved that they are simply awesome. The handsome statue of the Judge Bes is inscribed with hieroglyphs which date it from the reign of Pharaoh Psamtik I (7th century). Notice the life-like bronze statuettes of cats and kittens.

You don't have to know anything about numismatics to admire the large collection of gold and silver coins from ancient Greece. A 6th-century BC coin was minted by that noted gold enthusiast, Croesus. A set of medallions on show

Mr Five Percent

At the dawn of the Oil Age, a far-sighted Turkish-born Armenian put up money to help finance drilling in Mesopotamia (now Iraq), then part of the Turkish empire. Eventually he was to own five percent of the Iraq Petroleum Company.

Two world wars and the fuelling of millions of cars, planes and ships made Calouste Gulbenkian rich beyond imagination. He became an avid collector of antiquities and great art, beginning with Turkish and Persian carpets, Armenian and Arabic manuscripts and Greek and Roman coins. His passions spread to ancient Egyptian art, Chinese porcelain and Western painting, always looking for the most perfect examples in each of his chosen fields.

He was on his way to the United States when he fell ill in Lisbon. He was so impressed with his treatment here that he decided to stay, and established a philanthropic foundation to which he left most of his money and collections when he died in 1955. The Gulbenkian Museum is the result, along with many other cultural facilities in Portugal, including the Modern Art Centre, regional museums and educational institutes.

here may even have been prizes at the Olympic Games of AD 242.

A large section of the museum is devoted to the art of the Islamic East – ancient fabrics, costumes and carpets, plus ceramics, glassware and illuminated pages from the Koran. The picture windows show the fine art of landscaping, and the museum is surrounded by its own perfectly planned and maintained park.

The Gulbenkian Museum reflects the interests of its benefactor, including early Islamic glass.

The survey of Western art begins in the 11th century with illuminated parchment manuscripts. Tiny ivory sculptures of religious scenes come from 14th-century France, and there are some well-preserved tapestries from Flemish and Italian workshops of the 16th century.

Paintings by Dutch and Flemish masters include works by Hals, Van Dyck and Ruysdael. Pride of place is given to two Rembrandts: a portrait of a helmeted warrior believed to be Pallas Athene or Alexander the Great (probably modelled by Rembrandt's son Titus) and *Figure of an Old Man*.

The French collection has most strength in its furniture, tapestries and goldsmith's art from the 18th century, plus paintings by Boucher, Watteau and Fragonard. British art includes several works by Gainsborough and Turner.

An entire room is dedicated to the works of the 18th-century Venetian painter, Francesco Guardi. The collection of

19 *vedute* (views) and *capricci* (caprices) of Venice is generally considered to be the finest in existence.

The French Impressionists here are represented by Monet, Renoir, Degas and Manet. Two of the most charming works are Manet's *Boy with Cherries* and *Boy Blowing Bubbles*.

Just when you think Gulbenkian is running out of surprises, you discover that he was also something of an expert on Oriental art. The hall of Chinese porcelain starts with the Yuan dynasty (13th-14th century; around the time of Marco Polo) and goes on to some exquisite 17th- and 18th-century items. As is the case throughout the museum, each piece represents the pinnacle of a particular school of art, miraculously unmarred by the forces of time.

The last room of the museum must have been particularly close to Gulbenkian's heart. It contains 169 items by his friend René Lalique (1860-1945), the extremely versatile French jeweller who seems to catch the essence of the art nouveau movement. Here are pendants, bracelets, necklaces, brooches and combs of assorted materials and unexpected motifs – serpents, lovers, owls, crickets, beautiful women and butterflies. Each piece has its built-in charm.

The museum is only one element of the whole Calouste Gulbenkian Foundation. Elsewhere on the premises are concert and exhibition halls where choirs and ballets perform (see p.89), a library, a bookstore, a centre of modern art and an informal restaurant.

Museu Nacional de Arte Antiga
(National Museum of Ancient Art)

This museum is housed in a big palace improbably set on a hillside just above the Lisbon docks. If you get lost, ask for 'Janelas Verdes' (green shutters), the street it's on and also the name by which the palace and the museum of ancient art are better known. Of the many exhibits here, three in particular stand out.

The Adoration of St Vincent from Lisbon's convent of São Vicente de Fora (see p.31) is attributed to the 15th-century Portuguese master, Nuno Gonçalves. It contains recognizable portraits of contemporary dignitaries, including that of Henry the Navigator. Dozens of others are shown in every range of distraction – ire, boredom, amusement, and several of the assembled clergymen appear as ugly, evil or both.

The Temptation of St Anthony by Hieronymus Bosch was painted around 1500, and is a fantastic piece of Bosch hallucination, tempered with humour and executed with sheer genius. A crane rigged up like a helicopter, walking fish, animal-faced men and the most hideous disasters fill this unbelievably imaginative triptych.

A collection of 16th-century Japanese folding screens is the third star exhibit. You might miss these, in a small room all by themselves. The arrival of the Portuguese in Japan, seen through the eyes of the Japanese, is the theme of these extraordinary historical documents. Almost all the foreigners are portrayed as villains, while the locals, watching from their balconies, appear to be amused. Indeed who wouldn't be, at the sight of these strangely dressed, long-nosed grandees accompanied by fawning servants, folding chairs and even, in one case, sunglasses?

> **Signs:**
> *entrada livre*–
> **admission free**
> *é proibido tirar
> fotografias*–no
> **cameras allowed**

There's still much more to see: English, Flemish, Dutch, German, French, Italian and Spanish paintings of the 14th to 19th centuries, most meticulously restored – perhaps too new-looking to be wholly satisfying; china and glassware from Europe and the Orient; rare Portuguese furniture and tapestries; and a bequest by Calouste Gulbenkian – a room of ancient sculpture, up to his admirable standards, including a Greek torso of marble from the 5th century BC and a statue of a lion from the palace of Emperor Tiberius at Capri.

Museu Escola de Artes Decorativas (Decorative Arts Museum)

An old palace has been filled with the most choice pieces of furniture, ceramics, silver and carpets from 16th- to 19th-century Portugal and the Portuguese empire to form the Museu de Artes Decorativas. Fine examples of woodwork are arrayed in rooms that often look lived-in. Among the curiosities are: children's rooms with mini-furniture; a primitive version of a fold-up sofa-bed; and an 18th-century picnic basket fit for a very hungry king. The museum, and an attached school for bookbinders, cabinetmakers, engravers and other artisans, belongs to the Ricardo Espírito Santo Silva Foundation, which was established by the banker of the same name. The palace stands just above the Miradouro de Santa Luzia (see p.37), the lookout point from where you can survey the roofs of the Alfama area.

Convento da Madre de Deus (Convent of the Mother of God)

Although a bit out of the way (further along the waterfront from Praça do Comércio, past the Museu Militar), the convent contains one of Lisbon's most memorable churches as well as an important museum and is well worth the effort of getting there.

Founded at the beginning of the 16th century, the convent needed a top-to-bottom reconstruction after the earthquake of 1755. The interior of the restored church is overpoweringly rich. Someone had the original idea of covering the side walls with blue and white tiles from Holland; two rows of enormous paintings hang above them, and the ceiling is also full of paintings. Everywhere in the church the décor is a mixture of the most florid gilt woodwork, huge paintings and precious old tiles.

Museu do Azulejo (Azulejo Museum)

Devoted entirely to the art of painted tiles, the Museu do Azulejo occupies much of the building adjoining the splendid Convento da Madre de Deus, and includes a small double-decker cloister surrounded by tiles in Moorish-style geometric patterns. By official count about 12,000 *azulejos* are on show here, from 15th-century polychrome designs to 20th-century art deco.

Don't miss the *Great Lisbon Panorama*, a 36m (118ft) long picture composed of blue-and-white painted tiles, recording every detail of Lisbon's riverside as it looked 25 years before the 1755 earthquake. On a lighter note, seven whimsical panels show the great rags-to-riches story of an early 19th-century hatmaker.

Museu Militar (Military Museum)

On the site of a foundry where cannon were cast in the 16th-century, some of

Azulejos date from Moorish times. This one from the 17th century has kept its colours well.

the weapons now on show date back much further: cross-bows, maces and lashes; 14th-century mortars; even Vasco da Gama's two-handed sword, almost as tall as a man. The age of chivalry is represented by many suits of armour, custom-made for knights and their horses.

A large and nostalgic section specializes in World War I – photographs of Portuguese troops ready for battle at the front, faded uniforms, medals, bugles and helmets with huge bullet-holes as souvenirs. The patio of this building overflows with cannon and even a tank. The museum is a handy place to while away an hour if you're waiting for a train at the Santa Apolónia station, just across the square.

EXCURSIONS
Estoril Coast

The Costa do Estoril (formerly called Costa do Sol) begins just west of Lisbon and goes all the way around the tip of the peninsula to Guincho on the open Atlantic. Those seeking pollution-free swimming (see p.83) usually head for Guincho, but the famous old resort of Estoril itself, some 24km (15 miles) from Lisbon, is still worth a visit.

The half-hour train journey from Cais do Sodré station in Lisbon to Estoril goes through former fishing villages now turned into soulless commuter suburbs. If you go by the motorway (toll road) you will see nothing of them at all, but the coastal road still provides a scenic drive.

The railway station at **Estoril** is right alongside the beach. On the other side of the tracks (and across the coast road) is a formal park with disciplined ranks of colourful flower beds, shrubs, palm trees and ponds. The park constitutes the front lawn of the town's glitzy **casino**. With its nightclub, restaurants, bars, cinema, exhibition halls, shops and gaming rooms this is Estoril's one-stop after-dark amusement centre.

The rich and retired once had Estoril to themselves.
Now it lures summer crowds from Lisbon.

In spite of the modern décor this casino, which employs about 200 croupiers, maintains an old-fashioned pace. Gambling – roulette, blackjack, baccarat, craps and a typical Portuguese game known as French Bank – is suspended only two nights a year: Good Friday and Christmas Eve. Legend has it that somebody broke the bank one Good Friday, prompting a superstitious management to declare it a holiday thenceforth. (Officials dismiss the story as wishful thinking.) If you do feel like a flutter, then try your hand at any of the above or on one of the 300 or so slot-machines on your way out.

The rest of Estoril is as discreet as a big winner ought to be. Victorian villas and sleek modern mansions are tucked away behind green curtains of palms, eucalyptus, pines and vines. In the first half of the 20th century, many a dignitary and monarch, finding themselves either unexpected-

Blustery Cabo da Roca is as far west as you can go in mainland Portugal; to some it feels like the end of the world.

ly unemployed or exiled, gravitated to fashionable Estoril or Cascais to dream about restoration in luxurious privacy.

As early as the mid-18th century Estoril was attracting visitors because of its balmy climate and thermal spa baths, which were considered good for liver complaints. Long before that, however, prehistoric settlers had built a couple of cave-cemeteries, discovered in 1944 near the beach, dug out of the limestone. Along with skulls and bones and artefacts, four gold rings in a spiral design were found; you can see them at the museum in Cascais.

While Estoril is all resort – cosmopolitan and sybaritic – **Cascais** lives a double life. It has been called the small town of fishermen and kings, where men of the sea coexist peacefully with the retiring rich as well as camera-toting visitors.

Something is always going on at the local fishermen's beach, even on holidays when the little blue, yellow and red boats are in port or dragged up on the sand. A few fishermen in their Sunday suits trade vivid and interesting stories while local children turn the beach into a football field.

The workaday fishing scene attracts tourists who inspect the catch as it is unloaded from boats into wooden trays, and then rushed to the modern auction building. There the fish is sold by a reverse (Dutch) auction, in which the price starts high and decreases until somebody shouts a bid. You may not understand the chant of the auctioneer, but you'll like the look of what he's selling – lobster, shrimp, hake, squid and sardines. Retail sales are in the hands of local fishwives who set up stalls outside the market. For the finished product, try any of the dozen or so restaurants within walking distance of the beach.

The **main square** of Cascais is a charmer. The Paços do Concelho (the town hall) has stately windows with iron railings, separated by panels of *azulejos* depicting saints. The fire station occupies a place of honour between the town hall and an attractive church, while in the main square, with undulating designs in its mosaic pavement, stands a modern statue of King Pedro I.

The forbidding 17th-century fort, known as the *Cidadela* (citadel), is one of the few buildings to have survived the earthquake and tidal wave of 1755. In a small chapel within the walls is an image of St Anthony, traditionally borne on the back of a white mule during parades.

After an overdose of sun and salt, the municipal park down the road is a cool relief. Under towering trees swans preen their feathers alongside ponds brimming with plump red and silver fish. The palace in this park is a museum – the **Museu dos Condes de Castro Guimarães** – with archaeological remains, art works, old furniture, gold and silver. One prize exhibit is a 16th-century illuminated manuscript with a highly detailed picture of Lisbon harbour.

The road west passes **Boca do Inferno** (Mouth of Hell), a geological curiosity where in rough weather the waves send up astonishingly high spouts of spray accompanied by ferocious sound effects.

At **Guincho**, you have the choice of either a sandy beach or the rocks to fish from, but be careful, they face the open sea and it's often rough. Just up the coast you can see the windswept cape of **Cabo da Roca**, the most westerly point of mainland Europe.

Vacationers coming to the Costa do Estoril enjoy all the usual sports on land and sea as well as a very sophisticated nightlife. In addition, nowadays there are also some far more specialized events: car-racing, show-jumping, experimental theatre, a jazz festival and bullfights. The mean temperature on this coast is 21°C (70°F) in summer and 11°C (52°F) in winter: mild enough any time of year for a holiday.

 ### *Queluz*

If you feel like an easy half-day outing, head for Queluz, 14km (8 miles) west of Lisbon, and home to the pretty, pink palace taken by Junot as his headquarters during the Peninsular War (see p.20).

To get there you can either go on a coach tour or take a commuter train from Rossio station to Queluz. Alternatively drive yourself, leaving Lisbon on the motorway through the forest of Monsanto – the turn off is clearly signposted. You're hardly out of the mushrooming suburbs before you're alongside the elegant palace.

The **palace** was built in the second half of the 18th century under the direction of two very talented architects: Frenchman Jean-Baptiste Robillon and the Portuguese Mateus Vicente de Oliveira. As a working official residence for the royal family, Queluz thrived mostly during the reign of

Maria I (1777-99). However, the queen, best remembered for her madness, failed to enjoy the place during her frequent fits of depression.

From the road, the palace seems relatively unprepossessing, but Portuguese modesty is totally abandoned on the inside, where you will find a degree of shabby splendour. Not surprisingly, the **throne room** is the most lavish of all, with overpowering chandeliers and walls and ceilings layered with gilt. The Hall of Ambassadors has a floor like a huge chessboard, in addition to several mirrors, and

> **Fuel types for cars/trucks: unleaded (*sem-chumbo*), premium (*super*), diesel (*gasoleo*)**

thrones at the far end. Actually, Queluz is rather curiously laid out with public rooms bordering living quarters almost incoherently.

The **gardens** are the pride of Queluz and go on and on with clipped hedges in perfect geometric array and bushes barbered into inventive shapes. The huge old magnolia trees relieve some of the formality, while the orange trees close by are enough to keep any queen well supplied with marmalade (but don't pick the fruit – it belongs to the government!). Royal guests would usually enter the garden via the pompous but original **Escadaria dos Leões** (Lions' Staircase). The fountains in the garden include some surprising statuary, such as sea monsters with faces like Pekinese dogs. In the early 19th century dozens of live animals – not just dogs but lions and wolves – were boarded at Queluz, which was then the site of the royal zoo.

Queluz has one rather original attraction – an 'artificial' river. Enclosed between restraining walls covered in precious, painted *azulejos*, a real stream was actually diverted to pass through the huge palace grounds and was then dammed to raise the water level whenever the royal residents wanted a boat ride.

If you time your visit right, you can stay for lunch in the royal kitchen, which is now a large restaurant. With giant old utensils, a fireplace big enough for a crowd to walk into, and loads of atmosphere, the place is called, logically, *Cozinha Velha* – the old kitchen.

Most museums are closed on Monday, but Queluz takes Tuesday off – and any other day when visiting heads of state are in residence.

☞ *Sintra*

Sintra is a town worth writing home about. Situated 25km (16 miles) north west of Lisbon, it is the kind of place you visit for a day and yearn to return to forever. Up and down forested hillsides are clustered old palaces and stately homes from where there are several vistas. Even the local jail is in a castle. If you can climb high enough, you will see as far as the sea (though the climbing and the distance between these palaces means only the very hardy, with plenty of time, will explore on foot).

Start in the centre of town at the **Palácio Nacional** (also called the Paço Real, Royal Palace; closed on Wednesday). Except for its two huge conical chimneys, this might at first glance seem like a fairly ordinary hulk of a palace; but do not judge it by its sombre façade. A summer home for Portuguese kings since the early 14th century, the palace's design became more and more unpredictable and haphazard as wings were added over the centuries, with back-to-back medieval and Manueline style. The resulting interiors and furnishings are

Pena Palace, on a mountain top above Sintra,
is a 19th-century fantasy built for Queen Maria II.

remarkable and, among other treasures, contain some of the oldest and most valuable *azulejos* throughout all Portugal.

Every room in the Palácio Nacional has a story to tell. For instance, during the 17th century, the dull-witted Afonso VI was pressured into abdicating for the benefit of the country, therefore allowing his more effective brother, Pedro II, to become king. When a plot to restore Afonso to the throne was discovered, the former monarch was exiled to Sintra. For nine years, until he died in 1683, he was imprisoned in a simple room of the Palácio Nacional. It's said that the worn floor is a result of his constant pacing up and down.

A large and cheery hall tells a less tragic story. King João I (1385-1433) was caught in the act of kissing one of Queen Philippa's ladies-in-waiting. The king's response was to say '*por bem*' ('in a good cause'). Palace gossips had a field day until the king ordered the ceiling of the hall to be painted with magpies, as many as there were ladies-in-waiting, their mouths sealed with the motto '*por bem*'.

Several other ceilings are worth craning your neck for. One is decorated with pictures of 27 swans, each in a different position, while another has the traditional crests of noble families. There are also precious ceilings with intricate designs in the *mudéjar* style influenced by Moorish art.

As for those strange chimneys, shaped like upside-down ice-cream cones, they used to let the smoke out of the kitchen when oxen were being roasted for a couple of hundred visiting dignitaries.

Sintra's oldest monument, **Castelo dos Mouros** (Moorish Castle), hugs a rocky ridge overlooking the town. It was probably built during the 8th or 9th century, soon after the Moors occupied Portugal. The dauntless Afonso Henriques won it for the Christians in 1147 – a major victory in the reconquest of Portugal. Now the castle is just an old ruin, its crenellated walls still severe, but redundant with nothing behind to protect. It's only a 10-minute walk from the road, and well worth it for the views.

On the hilltop further up the same winding road, over 450m (1,500ft) above sea level, is the **Palácio da Pena**, an outrageous Victorian folly reached by way of a park so lush with flowering trees and vines it is like a tropical rainforest.

In 1511, King Manuel I ordered a monastery to be built on this site. It was mostly destroyed in the earthquake of 1755, though a notable chapel and cloister survive. The present, bizarre cocktail of Gothic, Renaissance, Manueline as well as Moorish architecture was designed as a love-nest for Queen Maria II (1834-53) and her romantic husband, Ferdinand of Saxe-Coburg-Gotha. Few have had the wealth to indulge their fantasies so grandly. The **view** from the terraces of this Disneyesque establishment sweeps all the way from the Atlantic to Lisbon. The palace is closed on Monday and public holidays.

If you can, go to Sintra on the second or fourth Sunday of the month, when a real country fair takes place in the adjacent village of São Pedro do Sintra – but be prepared for even worse traffic jams than usual. In the engrossing open market buy home-made bread, cheese and sausages, or even a bottle of patent medicine sold to you by an old-fashioned, slick-talking hawker. Antique collectors find many possibilities here, including religious statues, rustic furniture as well as ordinary 19th-century household appliances.

A final counsel: don't leave Sintra without buying at least one packet of *queijadas*, miniature cheesecakes in paper-thin crusts. These delightful and unique pastries may be the most delicate little cakes you come across throughout this sweet-toothed country.

South of Lisbon

Arrábida Peninsula

It's around 32km (20 miles) south from Lisbon over the bridge to the calm and clean seashore at **Sesimbra**. This is a working fishing town; in the morning the entire adult male population seems to be occupied on or near the beach, taking the knots out of the tough plastic fishing lines. The beach is narrow but quite long, and is sheltered from the brunt of Atlantic tides and harsh winds. Most of the tourist developments tend to merge fairly unobtrusively into the hillside.

Those **castle walls** silhouetted on the hilltop above Sesimbra are the genuine article, though recently restored. During the Middle Ages the whole town was situated up there, protected against sea raiders by the walls and the altitude. The Moors built the enclave, lost it to Dom Afonso Henriques in 1165, and won it back again for a few years before having to move out for good in 1200.

Not much is left inside the walls, but it's still worth the 6km (4 miles) ride up from the town below. A small but interesting archaeological museum is now set up in a room attached to the castle's 12th-century church, and the view down to the curve of the coast and back to the Arrábida mountains is magnificent. On the hill you pass three squat, white **windmills** – surprisingly, Portugal has more windmills than any other country in Europe (about 20,000, compared with fewer than 1,000 left in Holland).

The dreary, windswept promontory south west of Sesimbra ends at **Cabo Espichel**, a sailors' nightmare which attracts the most merciless Atlantic breakers. Although this is the perfect place for a lighthouse, it is also the unlikely setting for a sanctuary, Nossa Senhora do Cabo (Our Lady of the Cape). Pilgrims have been coming to this moody spot

*The high ridge of the Arrábida peninsula used to
be lined with windmills; a few are preserved.*

since the Middle Ages. The two rows of arcaded buildings
facing each other from across the front of the 17th-century
church were built to house them. Sadly, the whole ensemble
is now in a state of decay.

The topographical highlight of the Arrábida peninsula is
the Serra da Arrábida (site of a nature reserve), a mountain
chain around 35km (22 miles) long which protects the coast
from the strong north winds and accounts for the Mediterranean vegetation.

Setúbal, the district capital, is 20 minutes drive from
Lisbon by motorway, longer if you take the picturesque
route via Sesimbra and Arábida. The bus does it in an hour;
or you can take the ferry across the Tagus and then the train

– a total of an hour and a half. The train is likely to be a slow local service. By road or rail you can admire the olive and citrus country, with cows grazing among the trees – not at all the desolate terrain usually associated with olives. The farther south you go, the more significant the vineyards, with the Setúbal region producing a highly regarded Muscatel.

Setúbal is a conglomeration of market town, industrial centre, resort and Portugal's third largest fishing port. Narrow, inviting shopping streets twist through the centre of the city, and elsewhere there are more squares, monuments, statues and parks than a town of this size would normally boast.

Setúbal's greatest historical and artistic treasure, the **Igreja de Jesus**, was built around 1490 by the great French architect Boytac, who later built Lisbon's glorious Jerónimos Monastery (see p.41). A dramatic main portal leads into the church, which boasts two inspired elements of decoration: 17th-century *azulejos* on the walls, and stone pillars like twisted strands of clay, which appear somehow fragile-looking in spite of their obviously solid dimensions.

The monastery which adjoins the church has now been converted into the town museum, a mixture of early Portuguese paintings, archaeological odds and ends, and old furniture and tiles. The cloister was then reconstructed after the 1755 earthquake, but since then excavation has revealed parts of the original patio.

The 16th-century **fort** high above the town to the west is now a government-sponsored *pousada* (luxury hotel) with a dreamy sweeping view (see p.105). Down at the sea front, don't miss out on the action in the fishermen's quarter when brightly painted boats of all sizes return with fresh caught fish still wriggling.

Across the wide Sado River from Setúbal, the resort complex of Tróia has sprung up on a stretch of sand dunes with beaches so expansive that it will be almost impossible to keep them a secret forever. It's well over 100km (62 miles) away by land, but you can be there in just 5 minutes on a hovercraft from Setúbal. Alternatively, take a ferry boat.

To the North

Organized tours from Lisbon tend to use the major highways to save time. If you're driving yourself, you can meander more (though it may be slow going), taking in places such as the walled fortress of Óbidos (see p.71) and the popular seaside and fishing town of Peniche (see p.73).

All the excursion firms offer trips to Mafra (see below), as well as a long day's outing covering four major sites further north of Lisbon: the shrine of Fátima (see p.74), with two monasteries that capture the history and heart of Portugal, and the charming fishing town/resort of Nazaré (see p.77).

The 11-hour tour (which includes lunch, coffee and shopping breaks along the way) covers a lot of ground, much of it memorable. If you are travelling independently, you can cover all these at greater leisure, perhaps also making an overnight stop on the way; recommended places to stay are suggested in the hotels section of this guide (pp. 129-138).

Mafra

In modest Portugal the dimensions of the convent and palace of Mafra, 40km (25 miles) to the north west of Lisbon, are quite staggering. The frontage of the building, often likened to Spain's Escorial, measures over 220m (700ft). According to one count, there are around 7,000 windows and doors.

This monumental extravagance is attributable to King João V, who in 1711 conceived this project to celebrate the long-awaited birth of his first child, Princess D. Maria, after three years of marriage. The king hired a German architect with Italian experience named Ludwig (or Ludovice) to take charge of the project, which in total employed as many as 50,000 artists, artisans and labourers.

During the trip from Lisbon you will see ordinary country houses which are decorated all over – on walls, steps and patios – with mosaics of marble chips. This is marble country, which helps to explain the liberal use of it in the **basilica** of the Mafra complex. The original effects are best achieved by contrasting columns of white marble with, say, reddish marble walls. The statues are noteworthy, too.

The convent library has a vaulted ceiling and tall shelves housing 30,000 books, while its **hospital** is a bizarre church with 16 private sick-rooms all along the nave – so that patients could hear mass from their beds. In the old pharmacy, there's a gruesome display of primitive medical tools.

With luck you may be in Mafra on the day of a carillon concert, usually to be heard in late afternoon. Operated by an 18th-century Dutch machine the size of a house, the mellow tones of the bells can be enjoyed for miles around.

Most excursions go another 10km (6 miles) to the coast for lunch at the fishing village and expanding resort of **Ericeira**. The old part is a winsome town of cobbled streets winding between whitewashed cottages, everything clean, neat and treasured by both inhabitants and visitors alike.

Several restaurants overlook the beach and the Atlantic, and freshly caught fish is naturally a speciality.

Ericeira received its town charter around 750 years ago but scarcely attracted any attention until 1910, when Portugal's last king, Manuel II, hastily arrived from Mafra. In its little port, the king and his family boarded the royal yacht and sailed off to exile.

Óbidos and Peniche

North of Mafra, the town of **Torres Vedras** gave its name to the lines of defence running from the Atlantic to the River Tagus. A long series of hilltop strong points were built on Wellington's orders to protect Lisbon, and were held by his forces throughout the winter of 1810 (see p.21).

The French battered against them in vain, then were forced to retreat and eventually quit Portugal altogether. Dedicated students of military history can find traces of the Lines of Torres Vedras on the ridge above the town.

The town of Óbidos still has a circle of medieval walls. The castle is now a luxury pousada.

The place itself has a very attractive central square, but it's usually choked by traffic and you'll probably be grateful for the bypass. Vimeiro, nearer the coast, was the site of Wellington's second victory over the French invaders, at the start of the Peninsular War in 1807. Roliça, further north and close to the main road, was the first.

Almost too perfect to be true, the high medieval walls of **Óbidos** completely encircle a jewel of a town. Equally hard to believe, this was once a *coastal* fortress until the sea inlet here silted up, leaving the quiet Óbidos lagoon cut off and the shoreline nearly 10km (6 miles) away.

From the main parking area, you enter the town through a narrow southern gateway, partly lined with blue *azulejos*. A second way in at the north end is guarded by the 13th-century **castle**, with its high square and round towers. It's been adapted as one of the more luxurious *pousadas* (see p.20), but even if you aren't staying or eating in the restaurant, you can take a look and enjoy the view from the ramparts.

The narrow streets inside the walls are enchanting, all lined with whitewashed houses decorated with improbable quantities of flowers. Óbidos has probably never looked so neat and clean in all its history so it's inevitably jammed with curious visitors at times (come early or late in the day if you want to avoid the crowds).

It's a real pleasure just to stroll about, climbing up to the battlements and perhaps walking along the safer sections. Down at street level, Rua Direita runs from one gate to the other. Near the castle, the parish church, **Igreja de Santa Maria**, faces the main square. Take a look inside at its blue 18th-century *azulejos*, the odd blue-painted ceiling and the gilded tomb in the north wall. In the chapel to the right of the altar, the paintings of the life of St Catherine are by the Spanish-born Josefa d'Ayala. She came to live in Óbidos and the Portuguese have adopted her as their own: they usually call her Josefa de Óbidos. She died here in 1684, one of the first women in history to be recognized as a great artist.

Also facing the square, the **Museum** in the 16th-century town hall was set up by the Gulbenkian Foundation (see p.50). Laid out on three levels – don't miss the basements – a varied collection is well displayed and the religious and

*Bringing in the catch at Peniche, a scene
repeated at fishing ports up and down the coast.*

other statuary is very fine. The section on the Peninsular War
has weaponry from both sides and a clear topographical
model of the Lines of Torres Vedras (see p.71). Two maps
(one printed in London in 1790, one in Portugal in 1808) are
probably just like the ones used by Wellington to plan his
strategy.

Due west on the coast, the old port of **Peniche** was once
an island, but sand gradually accumulated and joined it to the
mainland to form the present peninsula. The imposing fortifications, built by Spain during its period of rule in the 16th
century, were meant to hold off pirates, or the English.
(Being the time of Sir Francis Drake, they were much the
same thing in Spanish eyes.)

It's worth collecting a town map at the tourist office,
which can also arrange accommodations – follow the signs
to *Turismo*. You'll find the **fishing harbour** usually jammed
with colourful, storm-battered craft and flanked by some excellent informal fresh fish restaurants. The **fort** nearby held

political prisoners during the Salazar régime; now it's a museum as well as a display area for local crafts and traditions. The huge sweep of sandy **beach** facing north is a local favourite. In fine weather (and calm seas unless you're immune to sea-sickness) you might like to take a trip to the island of **Berlenga**, 12km (7 miles) offshore. With monastery ruins and an impressive fort which still stands, it's now a sanctuary for innumerable seabirds.

Fátima

Set in bleak hill country about 135km (84 miles) north of Lisbon, this fast-growing town of smart apartment blocks and countless hotels was once just a poor village. Now it stands as one of the most important centres of pilgrimage in the Catholic world.

Its 20th-century neoclassical basilica faces a square said to be twice as big as St Peter's in Rome. This is where, in May 1917, three young shepherds saw a series of miraculous visions, followed by a solar phenomenon witnessed by thousands in October of the same year. Two of the children died soon after these inexplicable events; the third, Lucia, is a Carmelite nun in Coimbra. She makes very few public appearances now, although she was seen at the 50th anniversary ceremonies at Fátima, attended by Pope Paul VI and an estimated 2 million faithful from around the world.

Pilgrimages are held on the 13th of every month, with the most important observances in May and October. Yet even on an ordinary weekday crowds of believers, some kneeling in penitence, come to Fátima.

In spite of the nearby picnic grounds, car parking areas and dozens of religious souvenir shops, most of the usual gaudy trappings of a world-famous attraction have been successfully avoided.

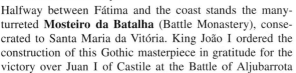

Batalha and Alcobaça

Halfway between Fátima and the coast stands the many-turreted **Mosteiro da Batalha** (Battle Monastery), consecrated to Santa Maria da Vitória. King João I ordered the construction of this Gothic masterpiece in gratitude for the victory over Juan I of Castile at the Battle of Aljubarrota nearby in 1385 (see p.15).

In the centre of the **Capela do Fundador** (Founder's Chapel), a tomb contains the remains of João and his queen, Philippa of Lancaster; their effigies lie side by side, hand in hand. Niches in the walls hold the tombs of their children, most notably that of Prince Henry the Navigator.

Still on a sepulchral note, Portugal's Unknown Soldiers are buried in the monastery's **Chapterhouse**. This vaulted chamber, 20m^2 (65ft), was a great engineering wonder in its

*Honey-coloured limestone is carved into
lace-like tracery at the 14th-century Batalha abbey.*

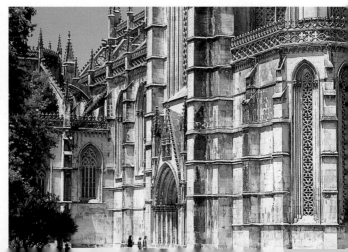

The peaceful cloister at Alcobaça, where Cistercian monks once walked in thought.

day (around 1400). Due to fears that the unsupported ceiling would collapse at any time, the architect is said to have employed only convicts under sentence of death to work on the project.

The **Claustro Real** (Royal Cloister), like the church, began as a Gothic work, but as construction continued after a couple of centuries the Manueline style was superimposed. Thus the columns and arches are decorated with the most unrestrained fantasies in filigreed stonework. By contrast, the carefully clipped hedges in the centre of the cloister are regimented in geometric patterns. Be sure not to miss the **unfinished chapels** attached to the east end of the church itself, but only attainable from the outside.

Older and bigger than Batalha is Abadia Real de Santa Maria, the former Cistercian monastery at **Alcobaça**. This, too, was built to celebrate a victory – the 1147 battle in which Dom Afonso Henriques took over the town of Santarém from the Moors. Though the exterior of the church has suffered centuries of architectural tinkering, the overall effect is still harmonious. The interior of unadorned limestone is very impressive; this is the biggest church in Portugal.

In the transept, about 30m (100ft) apart, are the **tombs** of Pedro I and his beloved Inês de Castro, their effigies surrounded by the figures of angels. The tombs are decorated with Portugal's greatest medieval stonecarving, depicting scriptural scenes. The delicate sculpture was damaged, mercifully not severely, by French soldiers looking for treasure when they sacked Alcobaça during their 1811 retreat. Inês was murdered for political reasons in 1355 having lived with Prince Pedro for ten happy years. When he became king just two years later, Pedro exhumed her body, crowned it, and ordered all nobles to kneel and kiss the skeleton's hand.

For a bit of relief from this tragic love story, be sure to visit the 18th-century kitchens with their huge tiled fireplaces. River water was channelled directly into the kitchen, so the monks could fill their tea kettles and catch their dinner at the same time.

Nazaré

The Portuguese 'Nazareth' is the fishing village you've seen in pictures. Although a thriving commercial resort now, some fishermen here still wear black stocking-caps and plaid trousers, and the women still appear in black shawls, bright aprons and seven petticoats (one for each day of the week – so it is said). Sadly, few of the traditional wide, flat-bottomed boats are left, and the oxen which used to pull them ashore have gone. Most fishing activity is concentrated at the new port on the town's southern outskirts.

Sítio, the 90m (300ft) cliff at the north end of Nazaré, is a supreme vantage point over the green hilly countryside, the tiled roofs of the neatly packed town, and mile after mile of **beach** open to the full force of the Atlantic Ocean.

In the old town behind the waterfront, many of the whitewashed houses have recently been transformed into restaurants, their tables half-blocking the narrow streets. During summer, thousands of tents fill the beaches, providing shade and shelter from the wind for the vacationers.

WHAT TO DO

SHOPPING

Lisbon is a sophisticated capital city, but one which at heart has not lost its old-fashioned feel. Shopping here runs to extremes – from chic boutiques to outdoor markets – and you can buy everything from expensive and intricate works of gold or silver to cheap trinkets. Either way, or somewhere in between, you should be able to find what you want.

When to Shop

Most shops are open Monday-Friday 9am-1pm and 3-7pm, and Saturday 9am-1pm. The 'commercial centres', modern shopping complexes, are usually open 10am-midnight or later, sometimes also on Sunday. Some of the Baixa shops also stay open during lunchtime. The Lisbon **flea market**, at Campo de Santa Clara, runs all day on Tuesday and Saturday. The vast **country market** at São Pedro de Sintra is held on the second and fourth Sunday of each month. Note: you may get away with haggling at antique stalls in the flea market, but it's not worth trying anywhere else.

What to Buy

Handicrafts excel in Portugal, but where do you start? Here are some shopping ideas:

Antiques: there is often a fine line between precious relics and plain, old-fashioned junk, but knowledgeable collectors will want to browse around the shops in Rua Dom Pedro V – the bustling street descending from the Rato to Cais do Sodré. If it's real nostalgia you're after, the flea markets are absolute gold mines. For the rustic touch, you might pick up a used cowbell or even a wagon wheel at village markets.

Azulejos: hand painted tiles have been decorating Portugal's walls throughout the centuries. You can buy a scene on a single blue-and-white tile or a batch to assemble into a picture when you get home. Some places will paint tiles to order if you have a particular design in mind, and some will copy a photograph.

Baskets: each region has its own way of weaving willow, rushes or straw into baskets for farm or home. The end result is strong,

Portuguese girls are taught the art of making lace from a young age.

useful and often very pretty, and, as a lightweight item, also comes with the bonus of posing no excess baggage problem.

Capes: in the Alentejo region, south of Lisbon, they still wear long cloaks in winter, usually in brown. Miniature models are delightful for children. You can also find traditional flowing capes.

Clothing: you might not find the same old bargains of the past, but Portugal is still a fairly low-cost producer of everyday casual clothing and fun sports wear.

Copperware: charming toy-sized pots and pans as well as conventional utensils, coffee sets and bric-a-brac.

Cork: Portugal is the world's leading producer of cork, and not only for those millions of wine bottles. You will also find decorative spin-offs such as intricate cork sculptures and lightweight souvenirs.

Dolls: these come in all sizes in authentic costumes.

Traditional crafts and modern, brightly coloured pottery can be found at Lisbon street stalls.

Embroidery: thousands of women on the beautiful island of Madeira produce world-famous needlework. The linen or organdie table-cloths are admirable but expensive; a handkerchief is a cheaper option. Hand-embroidered goods also come from the Azores and some mainland towns, notably Viana do Castelo. Do look out as well for intricate lace-work from the towns along the Portuguese coast.

Filigree: the Moors brought this beautiful style of art with them during the 8th century. The most unmistakably Portuguese design is a caravel made of gold or silver wire. Craftsmen also produce fine brooches in the form of flowers or butterflies.

Ironwork: though heavy on the baggage scales, flower-pot-holders, old-fashioned lamps and the like are certainly worth considering.

Knitwear: hand-knitted pullovers in sophisticated designs or chunky fishermen's jumpers are a must. Many come from either the north of Portugal or the Algarve.

Leather: belts, bags and shoes are still very popular buys.

Macau imports: Portugal's Chinese connection still supplies a great variety of shopping ideas, including genuine oriental tea sets, painted rice bowls, and even furniture.

Madeira wine: take home a bottle or two of this celebrated product of the sunny island's volcanic soil. It can be served either before or after dinner, as a dessert wine.

Oil paintings: Portuguese artists paint in varied styles. Fishing boats and seafaring folk are the usual favourite themes, along with typical scenes of the narrow twisting streets of the Alfama district.

Port: the legendary wine from the Douro Valley near Oporto in the north is best known as an after-dinner tradition, but also comes in aperitif versions (see p.96). Even in Portugal, really good port is an expensive hobby. For something a little more unusual, take home a bottle of white port.

> Sizes (*medidas*) may vary with the manufacturer. Make sure to try on shoes and similar items before buying.

Pottery: a long, distinguished but slightly mixed-up history starting with the Phoenicians accounts for the many different designs and colours of pottery that one can see and buy in Portugal, from fine porcelain to folksy earthenware.

Records and cassettes: take the sad and haunting lament of the traditional *fado* (see p.88) back home with you.

Roosters: statuettes in wood or ceramic, hand-painted in bright, gaudy colours, honour Portugal's fabled rooster. According to the residents of the northern town of Barcelos, where the figurines are all made, the indomitable bird actually rose out from a judge's dinner plate and crowed loudly to proclaim the innocence of an unjustly condemned man.

Rugs: beautiful bright colours and equally cheerful designs are the hallmark of rugs from Arraiolos, an Alentejo village with a three-century-old rug industry.

Shawls and scarves: if the sweeping black model used by *fado* singers isn't for you, look into the selection of brightly designed scarves.

Wickerwork: as well as baskets you'll also find handmade wicker chairs and tables, ship models and animal figures.

Yokes: oxen used them first, but now people have discovered that they make striking headboards or chair backs. Carved scale models are excellent as hat racks.

SPORTS

From the most simple pursuits, such as swimming and hiking, to the challenge of deep-sea fishing, sports enthusiasts can usually find what they're looking for in the Lisbon area. The gentle climate also means year-round golf and tennis.

If you're interested in diving or water-skiing, or any other sport for which you need to hire equipment, ask about the best places to do so at the tourist information offices in each town.

Diving: just off Sesimbra, the extraordinarily clear, calm waters favour snorkelling and scuba diving.

Fishing: all along the coast you will see anglers in boots casting off from the beaches, and others perched on rocks or man-made promontories. Most of them say business is good. The best deep-sea fishing is for swordfish around Sesimbra.

Golf: the Lisbon area has several courses including: Estoril Palácio Golf Club at Estoril (18 holes); tel. (01) 468 0176; Golf Estoril Sol near Sintra (9 holes); tel. (01) 923 2461; Lisbon Sports Club at Belas near Queluz (18 holes); tel. (01) 431 0077; Quinta da Marinha Golf and Country Club near Cascais (18 holes); tel. (01) 486 9881; and Tróia Golf Club near Sétubal (18 holes); tel. (065) 44112.

Riding: you can hire a horse, with or without an instructor, at the Lisbon Country Club or at one of several other riding academies in and around Lisbon, including the Quinta da Marinha Golf and Country Club, which also has an equestrian centre; tel. (01) 486 9282.

Self-catering? Coastal waters and northern rivers yield all types of fish, from sardines to lampreys.

Sailing and boating: most beaches which are protected from the open ocean have rowing boats, canoes or pedalos for rent by the hour. Experienced sailors in search of a more seaworthy craft should ask at the local yacht.

Swimming: because of pollution along the Estoril Coast, you should not swim any closer to Lisbon than at Estoril itself, which has been granted an EU blue flag. At Guincho and beyond the sea is perfectly clean and quite safe to swim in, but beware of the strong undertow. South of Lisbon from Caparica onwards is really delightful, but can also be windy, and with very rough seas. An immense stretch of beach on the Tróia peninsula can be reached from Setúbal by ferry or hovercraft.

Ask at the government tourist office for the leaflet on Portuguese beaches, with maps and details of facilities.

Tennis: major hotels tend to have their own tennis courts, but there are tennis clubs and public courts as well. Many golf clubs also have their own courts, as do the sports centres at Campo Grande in Lisbon and Tróia, opposite Setúbal.

Water-skiing: Estoril and Portinho da Arrábida (between Sesimbra and Setúbal) are the best places to try your hand at water-skiing.

Spectator Sports

Car racing: the Formula One Grand Prix takes place at Estoril's autodrome, on the road to Sintra, in late September.

Football (soccer): as in most countries, this usually draws big crowds in Portugal. Lisbon's two major teams are Benfica and Sporting.

Horse-racing: regulated since the 14th century by the government, horse-racing is still a very popular spectator sport. Lisbon's Campo Grande hippodrome in the north of the city (Metro: Cidade Universitaria) is usually the best place to go, but formal betting is no longer legal here. Races and polo matches are held at the equestrian centre at the Quinta da Marinha Golf and also at the Country Club (see Riding on p.82).

Dressage and jumping competitions are held at Cascais.

LISBON FOR CHILDREN

With its trams, elevators, funiculars and ferries, Lisbon offers some great ways to entertain the kids just by travelling around the city or across the River Tagus. The museums are a bit serious for younger children, but older ones may like the ship models at the Maritime Museum (see p.43) or the weaponry at the Military Museum (see p.55). The zoo (see p.48) is old-fashioned but makes an effort to entertain younger visitors with features such as elephant rides, boats and a miniature train.

For a safe beach with clean water you'll have to go some way from the city (see p.83). Head for Guincho and Caparica when the wind is light, or Sesimbra and Tróia otherwise. Caparica has a waterpark with long, twisting slides.

BULLFIGHTS

Children over six are admitted to Portuguese bullfights. You need have few qualms about taking yours to see the colour and drama of the *corrida* without the killing. The fights are less conclusive than the Spanish version – and more fun.

Eight bulls, each weighing nearly half a ton, will enter the arena in turn. Four are fought *à antiga portuguesa*, in the uniquely Portuguese way, and four are taken on by a matador who doesn't kill but dominates the bull with his cape, without the aid of picadors.

The four rounds *à antiga* contain elements of a circus, a horse-show and a rodeo.

Riding trams in town (above) or playing football on the beach, there's plenty for children to do.

85

The horses are fearless, high-stepping, loyal and agile. The bullfighters can maintain superb control over their huge mounts. Horse and rider are as one, teamed to arouse the bull, outrun and outwit him. During each chase the proud *cavaleiro* (horseman) stabs a long dart into the bull's shoulder. When the full quota of darts (*farpas*) has been inserted, the horseman salutes the crowd and leaves the field. In the second act, eight very brave young men leap over the fence onto the sand to face the bull on foot, ostentatiously unarmed. The bull's horns have been padded, but he can still inflict damage. The men on foot (*forcados*) subdue the bull with their bare hands. Or, at least, they try to.

Lisbon's Campo Pequeno bullring (Metro: Campo Pequeno) at the top of Avenida da Republica is a Victorian redbrick landmark with mock Moorish arches and bulbous domes. The arena in Cascais is bigger, but a bullfighter hasn't 'arrived' until he has won the esteem of all the loyal fans at Campo Pequeno.

The season runs from Easter Sunday to October. As with Spain, seats in the shade (*sombra*) cost more than in the sun (*sol*), though there are performances in the evening as well. For a modicum of comfort, rent a pillow from the usher.

FESTIVALS

Portugal's folk festivals are modest compared with such international attractions as the Carnival in Rio or the running of bulls in Pamplona. Tourist information offices will have a timetable of festivals and fairs around the country, which is worth checking as you plan your excursions.

Most of the colourful religious processions are confined to the north of the country. In towns around Lisbon the Patron Saint's Day may be celebrated both at church and with dancing in the streets, fireworks and bullfights.

CALENDAR OF EVENTS

As you plan your excursions, it is worth checking details of festivals and fairs around the country with tourist information offices.

May – Sesimbra: Festival of Senhor das Chagas procession (3-5 May).

Fátima: Pilgrimage (13 May).

June – Lisbon: Festival of music, dance and theatre. Concerts and performances.

Lisbon and elsewhere (especially in Alfama): Fairs and festivities for the 'People's Saints', honouring St Anthony (13 June), St John (24 June) and St Peter (29 June).

July – Sintra: Music Festival, live performances in the town's historic palaces and gardens.

Vila Franca de Xira (north of Lisbon): Running of bulls in the streets; (first two Sundays of the month).

July-August – Estoril/Cascais: Estoril International Music Festival.

Estoril: Open-air craft fair every evening.

Setúbal: Festival of Santiago, fair and exhibition.

August – Peniche: Festival of Our Lady of the Good Voyage.

September – Palmela: Wine Festival, parades, tastings and fireworks (mid-Sep).

Nazaré: Festival of Our Lady (second week in September).

Cabo Espichel: Festival of Our Lady of the Cape (last Sunday).

October – Vila Franca de Xira: Fair, running of bulls (first Sunday).

Fátima: Pilgrimage (13 October).

Óbidos: Early Music Festival (2nd week of October).

Moveable Dates: Check dates with tourist information offices.

February-March – Towns around the country: Carnival (Mardi Gras). Processions and fireworks.

March-April – Towns around the country: Holy Week. Palm Sunday, Good Friday and Easter Day services and processions.

Carnival time in Lisbon is a rather subdued affair. Fire-crackers go off in the streets, but pre-Lenten festivities on the whole tend to be confined to private parties.

June is the month of Lisbon's popular saints – Anthony, John and Peter. Fairs are held in the neighbourhoods with folk dancing sports competitions and exciting firework displays. The biggest day is 13 June, honouring the local boy who grew up to be St Anthony of Padua (see p. 34).

ENTERTAINMENT

Even if you're not really the nightclub type, you'll still find something to occupy your evenings in Lisbon.

Don't miss a rousing night out at one of the *fado* houses in Alfama or the Bairro Alto. A century ago 'respectable' people were reluctant to be seen in a *fado* club; nowadays the danger is not to your reputation, only to your pocket – tickets are quite expensive. Inclusive tours are available.

Casas de fados or adegas típicas are restaurants where you eat or drink to the sound of the fado.

The dramatic atmosphere of a **fado** house adds to the impact. Guitarists start off the proceedings with a warm-up number. Then the lights dim, the audience goes quiet, and a strong spotlight picks out a woman in black who wails out a song of tragedy and despair. Her sultry voice sums up that most Portuguese emotion, *saudade* – longing, regret, nostalgia. It can send a shiver down your spine.

The majority of *fado* singers are women, but you may hear a man perform the same sort of ballad with a strong, husky voice and tragic mannerisms. The *fado* is never danced – it's much too solemn. Instead, regional fishermen's and shepherds' dances are sometimes performed to perk things up.

In Lisbon's Bairro Alto you can also find conventional discos, nightclubs, jazz clubs and bars for all tastes, some open until 5am.

Music: Lisbon's cultural scene offers occasional opera, symphony concerts, ballet and recitals, usually held in winter. The city's opera company is highly regarded by the rest of the world, and the Gulbenkian Foundation (see p.50) maintains its own symphony orchestra and ballet company.

> **Signs:**
> *entrada*–entrance
> *saída*–exit
> *chegada*–arrival
> *partida*–departure

Portugal has three other important symphony orchestras and a national dance company. Soloists and ensembles from many countries also perform here. Check at your hotel desk or the government tourist office to find out what's on.

Theatre and cinema: most of Lisbon's stage plays are comedies and revues - in Portuguese, of course. Cinemas tend to show foreign films in the original language with Portuguese subtitles.

Two publications, *Diário de Notícias* and the weekly *Se7e*, (see p.118) contain the most complete music, stage and screen listings, including times of performances.

Gambling: if you're not very familiar with the main rules of roulette, the Portuguese game French Bank, baccarat, craps or blackjack, the Estoril Casino (see p.56) issues illustrated instruction leaflets, in English and Portuguese. After that you are on your own.

To enter the gaming rooms you have to pay a fee and show your passport. The casino is open 3pm-3am daily (except Good Friday and Christmas Eve). A sign 'suggests' that gentlemen wear jackets after 8pm, but no rules are enforced. After a good win, it's customary to flip a chip or two to the croupier.

EATING OUT

The only problem in Portuguese restaurants is the size of the portions – simply gargantuan. With a little practice, though, you'll soon be coping – and if not, then feel free to ask for a half portion (which is usually charged at around two-thirds the full price).

Seafood fans are in luck here, revelling in the taste of just-caught fish and shellfish. Not that the menus skimp on meat: you can find delicious pork and lamb dishes and even a presentable steak. You'll also enjoy the flavour of freshly picked fruit and vegetables, not to mention the variety of Portuguese wines, which are eminently drinkable.

Where to Eat

Government inspectors rate all Portuguese restaurants on a scale of four categories. In descending order they are *de luxo* (luxury), *de primeira, de segunda* and *de terceira classe* (first, second and third class). The higher the rating, the more the restaurant is permitted to charge. A sign showing the class is often displayed outside restaurants, while menus displayed in the window or beside the door let you know what to expect in variety and price. Prices normally include taxes and a service charge, but you can leave an additional 5-10% tip for very good service.

Whether you live it up in the most elegant establishment or test the local colour in a humble fishermen's hangout (this is often where you'll find the best food), you are likely to come across a whole variety of dishes you've never heard of before.

Buyer Beware

Today, many restaurants and cafés offer an *ementa turística*, quite literally 'tourist menu', but this is not meant just for

The landmark Cafe Nicola where paintings recall the life of the poet Bolage (1765-1805).

passing tourists. It is an economically priced set meal, typically bread, butter, soup, main course (or a choice of two) and dessert. Do watch out though: if you deviate even slightly from it you may be charged à la carte prices for each item. Likewise, the prices displayed outside some of Lisbon's cafés only apply if you stand at the bar. In Portugal, as in other European countries, if you sit down you will have to pay the higher prices quoted on the regular menu.

Remember that nothing ever comes free. Generous appetizers are often scattered on your table: what you eat you pay for. Also, in restaurants where seafood portions are generally charged by weight, the dishes may keep coming and if you don't say stop soon enough, the bill can be quite a shock.

Meal Times

Breakfast (*o pequeno almoço*) is usually eaten any time up until about 10am. **Lunch** (*o almoço*) is served from shortly after noon until 3pm, and **dinner** (*o jantar*) runs from 7.30 to 9.30pm (or later in a *casa de fado*). In-between-meal snacks may be found at a *pastelaria* (pastry and cake shop) or *salão de chá* (tea shop), or what the Portuguese call a *snack bar* – a stand-up counter selling sandwiches, savoury pastries, and sweet things.

Because lunch and dinner tend to be major events, you may prefer the kind of light breakfast the Portuguese eat: coffee, toast or rolls, butter and jam. Hotels can provide all the extras – juice, cereal, eggs, bacon – frequently on a buffet.

Soups

Lunch and dinner often get off to a hearty start:

Caldo verde (green soup): a distinctive Portuguese soup – a thick broth of potato purée with finely-shredded cabbage or kale. Sometime sausage is added.

Sopa à Portuguesa: a similar soup to *caldo verde*, but with added broccoli, turnips, beans, carrots and anything else the cook happened to have on hand.

Sopa de cozido: a rich meat broth with cabbage and perhaps macaroni added. (This is often followed by *cozido* – a huge serving of all the things that were boiled to create the broth, including beef, chicken, pork, sausages, potatoes, cabbage and carrots.)

Canja de galinha: chicken and rice soup.

Note: Portuguese cooks are so confident of their seasoning that salt and pepper are seldom put on the table. You will be given them if you ask, though – '*sal e pimenta, por favor*' – and the chef won't sulk.

From the Deep

The best advertisement for seafood is usually in the window of a restaurant – a refrigerated display case with crabs and prawns, oysters and mussels, sea-bass and sole. Seafood restaurants generally sell shellfish by weight, giving the price in escudos per kilo.

Amêijoas na cataplana: an invention from the Algarve, of steamed mussels (or clams) with sausages, tomato, white wine, ham, onion and herbs.

Açorda de marisco: a spicy, garlic-scented bread-soup full of seafood bits; raw eggs are later folded into the mixture.

Lulas recheadas: squid stuffed with rice, olives, tomato, onion and herbs.

Lampreia à Minho: a bed of rice and a red wine sauce beautify the unlovely lamprey, quite a delicacy in Portugal (best from January to March).

Bacalhau: Cod is the national dish of Portugal, even though it can be expensive and comes dried and salted and from distant seas (which is quite odd, because some of the tastiest fresh fish in the world is right on the doorstep).

Depending on which tale you believe, cod is served in 100, 365 or 1,000 different ways. It has to be said, *bacalhau* is something of an acquired taste. The best way to try it – because you can't really taste it – is in *Bacalhau à Gomes de Sá*, in which flaky chunks are baked with parsley, potatoes, onion and olives and garnished with grated hard-boiled egg.

Fresh fish, whole or filleted, is usually served grilled, as are outstanding *atum* (tuna) and *espadarte* (swordfish steaks). The Portuguese are also very fond of boiled fish dishes, usually served with generous portions of cabbage and boiled potatoes and doused with a little oil and vinegar.

Meat

Bife na frigideira: this is not what you might think. *Frigideira* means frying pan, and this dish is a beefsteak nicely done in a wine sauce.

Cabrito assado: baked goat kid served with rice and potato, heavy going but delicious.

Carne de porco à Alentejana: an inspired idea, clams and pork cooked with paprika and garlic.

Espetada mista: Portuguese shish kebab – chunks of beef, lamb and pork on a spit.

Feijoada: a far cry from the more elaborate national dish of Brazil, but still a really filling and tasty stew of pigs' trotters and sausage, white beans and cabbage.

The freshest fish, simply grilled and served in the open air.

Most meat dishes in Portugal are served with *both* rice and potatoes.

Portuguese menus can often be unintentionally misleading when foreign names are used. Chefs dub favourite recipes 'à provençal' or 'à Yorkshire' or whatever else sounds exotic, but the dish may have no connection at all with the usual gastronomic interpretation.

Game and Fowl

Chicken – *frango* – is popular cooked in many ways: stewed in wine sauce, fried, roast and barbecued to a tasty crisp.

Some restaurants specialize in game – *codorniz* (quail), *perdiz* (partridge), *lebre* (hare) and even *javali* (wild boar).

Dessert and Cheese

The national sweet tooth may be a little too much for your taste. After all, where else do people pour sugar on a sliced sweet orange? The cakes, custards and pastries – an endless variety, but usually made with egg yolks and sugar – are really delicious.

Pudim flã (*flam, flan, flão*): the Portuguese version of the Spanish *flan* (caramel custard).

Arroz doce: rice pudding with a dash of cinnamon.

Maçã assada: tasty sugary baked apple.

Pudim Molotov: no one is quite certain about the derivation of the name, but it's surely the richest dessert to explode any strict diet. The fluffy egg-white mousse is immersed in a sticky caramel sauce.

All of this may deflect you toward cheese. The richest and most expensive in Portugal is *Serra da Estrela*, a delicious cured ewes' milk cheese from high up in the mountains. Also on many of the menus is *Flamengo*, a mild cheese and very similar to Edam. Some restaurants serve *quiejo fresco* as an appetizer. This is quite a small, white, soft mini-cheese made of ewe's and goat's milk, and is so bland you'll want to add pepper and salt.

International Dishes

Thanks to Portugal's imperial memories, you can experiment while you're in Lisbon. The former colony of Goa accounts for the local popularity of *caril* (curry) and other Indian-style dishes. A typical Goan delicacy, a lot less pungent than Indian food, is *xacuti* (pronounced and sometimes spelled *chacuti*). This is simply chunks of fried chicken in a sauce of pepper, coriander, saffron, cinnamon, cumin, anise, cloves, and coconut milk, served with steamed rice.

Four centuries of ties with the territory of Macau assures all lovers of Chinese food a night out with dishes such as *gambas doces* (sweet-and-sour prawns) and all the fixings.

Table Wines

Portugal is one of those fortunate countries where all you need to tell the waiter is *tinto* (red) or *branco* (white) and you can't go wrong. If the choice of white or red isn't broad enough, you can order pink or green.

Port from Portugal ...

Thanks to the unique growing conditions of the Douro Valley in the north of Portugal, port wine has tantalised palates around the world since the British started exporting it in the 17th century. It differs from other wines due to the climate and soil, and to the fact that the fermentation process is stopped with brandy.

Around 10 percent of the grapes picked each year are still crushed in treading rooms by barefoot men. After two or three days' fermentation the brandy is added. The following spring, the fortified wine is sent to mature at the lodges on the banks of the River Douro at Vila Nova de Gaia (opposite Porto), from where it is shipped.

... and Madeira from Madeira

First produced on the island of Madeira in the 15th century, Madeira wine became an important export trade due to a combination of its notable quality and Madeira's position on the shipping lanes to the Indies. With the rise of the British colonies in North America and the West Indies, it fast became a favourite on both sides of the Atlantic.

Madeira wine only became a fortified wine when it was decided to add grape brandy in order to stabilize it on long sea voyages.

Vinho verde ('green wine'), produced in the north-west, is a young white wine, semi-sparkling and thoroughly delightful. A lesser known type is red wine from the same region, bearing the improbable name *vinho verde tinto* ('red green wine'). Both these wines should be served chilled, as should Portuguese rosé, which is also slightly bubbly and may be either sweet or very dry.

Vinho espumante is Portuguese sparkling wine, packaged in a Champagne-shaped bottle. Most are sweetish but you can also find some quite dry versions.

Several wine-producing regions near Lisbon have names whose use is controlled by law. You may come across these classifications:

Bucelas – a light and fresh white wine; *Colares* – a traditional red wine; *Setúbal* – mellow, sweet white, sometimes served as an aperitif.

Dão in the north of Portugal produces vigorous reds and flavourful whites.

Other Drinks

The two most celebrated Portuguese wines, port and Madeira, are mostly known as dessert wines, but they may also be sipped as aperitifs. The before-dinner varieties are dry or extra dry white port and the dry Madeiras, *Sercial* and *Verdelho*. These should be served slightly chilled. After dinner, sip one of the famous ruby or tawny ports, or a Madeira dessert wine, *Boal* or *Malvasia* (Malmsey).

Portuguese beers are good. Light or dark, they are served chilled, bottled or from the tap. *Aguardente* is the local brandy.

You can find various brands of mineral water in small or large bottles, bubbly or still. Portuguese fruit juices can be delicious, and well-known soft drinks are also available.

Coffee and Tea

At the end of lunch or dinner, most people order a *bica*, a small cup of black espresso coffee. Curiously, a diluted black coffee is called a *carioca* – even though the Cariocas (inhabitants of Rio de Janeiro) drink theirs infinitely stronger. Cafés also serve weaker, white coffee, usually made with hot milk; in a tall glass it's called a *galão*, in a small one, a *garoto* ('little boy').

> *À sua saude!* (ah sooer serooder)– cheers, literally "to your health"

Tea (*chá*) is still a very popular drink in Portugal; after all, it was the Portuguese explorers who first introduced it to the rest of the Western world. Although the concept of afternoon tea is regarded as British, its origins are Portuguese, dating from 1662, when Catherine of Bragança, sister of Dom Afonso VI, married the English King Charles II. Her fashionable court popularized tea drinking.

To Help You Order ...

Could we have a table? **Queríamos uma mesa.**
Do you have a set-price menu? **Tem uma ementa turística?**
I'd like a/an/some ... **Queria ...**

beer	**uma cerveja**	napkin	**guardanapo**
bill	**a conta**	potatoes	**batatas**
bread	**pão**	pork	**porco**
butter	**manteiga**	salad	**uma salada**
chicken	**frango**	salt	**sal**
dessert	**sobremesa**	sandwich	**sanduíche**
fish	**peixe**	shellfish	**mariscos**
fruit	**fruta**	soup	**uma sopa**
ice-cream	**um gelado**	sugar	**açúcar**
lamb	**borrego**	meat	**carne**

menu	**a ementa**	tea	**chá**
milk	**leite**	vegetables	**legumes**
mineral water	**água mineral**	wine	**vinho**

... and Read the Menu

alho	garlic	**gambas**	prawns
almôndegas	meatballs	**guisado**	stew
ameijoas	baby clams	**lagosta**	spiny lobster
ananaz	pineapple	**laranja**	orange
arroz	rice	**limão**	lemon
assado	roast	**linguado**	sole
atum	tuna	**lombo**	fillet
bacalhau	codfish	**lulas**	squid
besugo	sea bream	**(à sevilhana)**	(deep-fried)
bife (vaca)	beef steak	**melancia**	watermelon
biscoitos	biscuits	**mexilhões**	mussels
bolo	cake	**molho**	sauce
caracóis	snails	**morangos**	strawberries
caranguejo	crab	**ostras**	oysters
cavala	mackerel	**ovo**	egg
cebola	onion	**pescada**	hake
chouriço	spicy sausage	**pescadinha**	whiting
coelho	rabbit	**pimento**	green pepper
cogumelos	mushrooms	**polvos pequenos**	baby octopus
couve	cabbage		
dobrada	tripe	**presunto**	ham
dourada	sea-bass	**queijo**	cheese
enguias	eel	**salmonete**	red mullet
ervilhas	peas	**salsichão**	salami
feijões	beans	**torrada**	toast
flã	caramel	**truta**	trout
framboesas	raspberries	**uvas**	grapes
frito	fried	**vitela**	veal

INDEX

Where there is more than one set of references, the one in **bold** refers to the main entry. Page numbers in *italic* refer to an illustration.

BERLITZ TRAVEL TIPS

An A–Z Summary of Practical Information

Listed after most main entries is an appropriate Portuguese translation, usually in the singular. You'll find this vocabulary useful when asking for information or assistance.

A

ACCOMMODATIONS (See also CAMPING on p.106, YOUTH HOSTELS on p.128 and RECOMMENDED HOTELS on pp.130-138)

Except for the family-run *hotéis rurais*, hotels in Portugal are graded from 2-star to 5-star deluxe. Rates are lower in less elaborate hosteleries: an *estalagem* or inn; a *pensão* (rooms with meals available); or *residencial* (rooms, generally without meals).

Pousadas (like Spanish *paradores*) are state-run establishments in historic buildings and scenic sites, aimed at acquainting visitors with traditions in different parts of the country. Special attention is given to local food and wine as well as to the architecture and handicrafts of the region. Ask at tourist offices (see p.123) for the detailed list.

Accommodation is also available in private houses (*turismo de habitação*), often estates or farms in areas where hotels are scarce, particularly in the north. Some establishments offer room and breakfast only, while others provide meals, tennis, horse riding and other sports as well. Tourist offices will have further details.

When you arrive at your accommodation, you'll usually be asked for your passport and to sign a form which sets out the conditions, prices and room number. Breakfast may be included in the total cost.

a double/single room	**um quarto duplo/simples**
with/without bath	**com/sem banho**

AIRPORT (*aeroporto*)

The Aeroporto de Lisboa (also known as Portela, the suburb where it's located) is only a 15-minute drive from the centre of Lisbon (allow twice as long at rush hour). Facilities include a bank, car-rental desks, tourist office, bars and a restaurant, souvenir stands, an the duty-free shop, as well as porters and free baggage trolleys.

Besides taxis, which are plentiful (see TRANSPORT on p.124), yo can take bus 44 or 45 for Cais do Sodré station (abbreviated 'C Sodré') about every 15 minutes during the day and every 25 minute in the early morning and late evening. They pass through the cit centre, including the Rossio. From Cais do Sodré station buses to the airport are marked 'Moscavide' (44) and 'Prior Velho' (45). Gree buses (*Linha Verde*) link the airport with Santa Apolónia station.

For information on flight times call 80 20 60; the main airpor number is 848 11 01.

Where do I get the bus to the airport/to the centre of Lisbon?	**Onde posso apanhar o autocarro para o aeroporto/ para o centro da cidade?**

C

CAMPING

Portugal has around 70 campsites, several in the Lisbon area, such as at Monsanto Park (see p.47). Facilities range from the basic to the elaborate (swimming pools, tennis courts, bars and restaurants).

To stay in the organized camping spots you must show your passport and an official card identifying you as a member of a national or international camping association. You cannot camp within city limits, or on beaches or other public places, nor light fires in forests.

Information on camping can be obtained from the tourist office (see p.123), or the Federação Portuguesa de Campismo, Av. 5 de Outubro no. 15, 3rd Floor; tel. 315 27 15, fax 54 93 72.

May we camp here?	**Podemos acampar aqui?**
We have a caravan (trailer).	**Nós temos uma roulotte.**

CAR RENTAL (*carros de aluguer*) (See also DRIVING on p.110 and PLANNING YOUR BUDGET on p.119)

International and local firms operate in Lisbon and major tourist areas. The minimum age for hiring a car is generally 21 (25 for some

rms), and you must have a valid licence, held for at least one year. If
ou present a recognized credit card the cash deposit will be waived
1 return for a signed credit card voucher. If the car is provided with a
ull fuel tank, you may be asked for a small deposit, returnable if the
ank is equally full when you bring the car back. Third-party insur-
ince is included in the basic charge but a collision damage waiver
and personal accident policy may be added.

'd like to hire a car today/ omorrow.	**Queria alugar um carro para hoje/amanhã.**
or one day/a week	**por um dia/uma semana**
lease include full insurance.	**Que inclua um seguro contra todos os riscos, por favor.**

CLIMATE and CLOTHING

Lisbon has an Atlantic climate influenced by the Mediterranean,
which offers hot summers and mild winters when there's a good
chance of rain. Spring and autumn are the best seasons to be in Lisbon, but in the summer, you can bask in the sunshine at the beaches.

	J	F	M	A	M	J	J	A	S	O	N	D
Air temperature												
°C	12	12	14	15	18	21	23	24	22	18	15	13
°F	54	54	57	59	64	69	73	75	72	64	59	55
Sea temperature												
°C	15	16	17	18	19	21	21	20	19	18	16	14
°F	59	61	62	64	66	69	69	67	66	64	61	57

Clothing (*roupa*).
Unless you come to Lisbon in an unseasonably cold winter, you'll
never really have to dress warmly. Spring and autumn are relatively
balmy, so you won't need anything heavier than a sweater in the day-
time. Summer days can be quite hot, but pack a wrap for cooler,
windy evenings and rainwear just in case.

Nowadays, virtually no establishment requires a tie. The Estor Casino 'recommends' that men wear jackets in the evenings.

Will I need a tie?	**E preciso gravata?**
Is it all right if I wear this?	**Vou bem assim?**

COMMUNICATIONS (See also TIME DIFFERENCES on p.123)

Post Offices (*correios*). Lisbon's mail service is quite efficient. Mail boxes follow the British pillar-box design and are painted bright red

Local post offices open Mon-Fri 9am-7pm. Major branch office also operate on Saturday until noon. A 24-hour office can be found a the airport. Lisbon's main post office in Praça dos Restauradores (op posite the tourist office) opens 8am-midnight daily. You can buy stamps from tobacconists' as well as at post offices.

You can have mail sent to you **poste restante** in any town. If you are in Lisbon, specify the main post office thus: Jane Jones, Posta Restante, Praça dos Restauradores 58, 1200 Lisbon, Portugal. Take your passport to pick up mail at the poste restante window. You will be charged a small handling fee for each letter received.

Have you received any mail for …?	**Tem correio para …?**
A stamp for this letter/postcard, please.	**Um selo para esta carta/este postal, por favor.**
express (special delivery)	**expresso**
airmail	**via aérea**
registered	**registado**
poste restante	**posta restante**

Telephones (*telefone*) **and fax**. Portugal's telephone system, although improving, may require considerable patience. Head for the post office and make your call from one of the official booths. Make your call and then pay for it at the counter.

Public telephones are usually found in British-style phone boxes booths). Coin boxes take 50, 20 and 10 esc coins; unused coins are eturned. Card phones (*Credifone*) can be purchased at post offices.

For international direct dialling, use 00 (both Europe and overseas; eg UK 0044, USA 001), followed by the area code (without the initial '0', where there is one) and subscriber's number. Dial 099 for he international operator for Europe, 098 for the rest of the world.

Post offices handle long-distance telephone, telegraph and telex services. The Marconi Company at Rua S Julião 131 operates a 24-hour service for international communications. Larger hotels and business services can send faxes for you.

reverse-charge call	**paga pelo destinatário**
Can you get me this number in …?	**Pode ligar-me para este número em …?**
I want to send a telegram to …	**Quero mandar um telegram a para …**

COMPLAINTS (*reclamação*)

Complaints should be addressed to the management of the establishment concerned, or to the head office of the department of tourism at Av António Augusto de Aguiar 86, 1100 Lisbon; tel. 57 52 86. Bring documents along to support your claim where possible.

CRIME AND THEFT (*delito*)

(See also EMERGENCIES on p.114 and POLICE on p.121)

It's always wise to keep your valuables in the hotel safe. Report any theft to the hotel receptionist, the nearest police station or the local tourist office. Bag-snatching has become more frequent, so carry your handbag firmly under your arm. Beware of pickpockets on buses, trams and in cafés in the Rossio Square, the Alfama area and other tourist spots. Leave nothing of value in parked cars.

I want to report a theft.	**Quero participar um roubo.**

Lisbon

CUSTOMS (*alfândega*) and ENTRY FORMALITIES

American, British, Canadian and many other nationalities need only a valid passport – no visa – to visit Portugal. This requirement i waived for the British, who may enter on a Visitor's Passport. Othe EU nationals may enter with an identity card. The length of stay au thorized for tourists is 90 days (60 for US citizens).

Currency restrictions. Visitors from abroad can bring any amoun of local or foreign currency into Portugal, but sums exceeding the equivalent of 1,000,000 esc in foreign currency must be declared or arrival. When leaving the country, you may take out foreign currency up to the amount imported and declared. No more than 100,000 escudos in local money may be exported per person per trip.

Customs. As Portugal is part of the EU, free exchange of non-duty free goods for personal use is permitted between Portugal and the UK and Eire. However, duty free items still are subject to restrictions: check before you go. For residents of non-EU countries, restrictions are as follows: **Australia**: 250 cigarettes **or** 250g tobacco; 1l alcohol; **Canada**: 200 cigarettes **and** 50 cigars **and** 400g tobacco; 1.1l spirits **or** wine **or** 8.5l beer; **New Zealand**: 200 cigarettes **or** 50 cigars **or** 250g tobacco; 4.5l wine **or** beer **and** 1.1l spirits; **South Africa**: 400 cigarettes **and** 50 cigars **and** 250g tobacco; 2l wine **and** 1l spirits; **USA**: 200 cigarettes **and** 100 cigars or a 'reasonable amount' of tobacco.

I've nothing to declare.	**Não tenho nada a declarar.**
It's for my personal use.	**É para uso pessoal.**

D

DRIVING IN LISBON (See also CAR RENTAL on p.106 and EMERGENCIES on p.114)

If you take your own car, you need your national driving licence, registration papers and insurance – third-party cover is obligatory. The Green Card makes it valid in other countries.

Driving conditions. The rules of the road are the same as in most western European countries. At roundabouts (traffic circles) the vehicle in the circle has priority unless road markings or lights indicate otherwise. Local driving standards are improving but are still erratic. Seat belts are compulsory. In towns, pedestrians nominally have priority at zebra crossings – but if you're walking, don't bank on it!

Speed limits. 120kph (75mph) on motorways, 90kph (56mph) on other roads and 50kph (37mph) in built-up areas. Minimum speeds are posted (in blue) for some motorway lanes and the suspension bridge across the River Tagus. Cars towing caravans (trailers) are restricted to 50kph (31mph) in towns and 70kph (45mph) on the open road and motorways (*portagem*). Most motorways have tolls.

Parking regulations. You have to park facing the same direction as the flow of traffic on that side of the road. Unless there's an indication to the contrary, you can park for as long as you wish. Certain areas are metered and others are 'Blue zones', where you must buy a ticket from a machine. Car parks and garages are also available.

Repairs. If you belong to a motoring organization affiliated to the Automóvel Clube de Portugal (Rua Rosa Araújo 24; tcl. 356 39 31) you can use their emergency and repair services free of charge. Otherwise, most garages in Portugal can handle the usual problems.

Road signs. Standard international pictograms are used in Portugal, but you might also encounter the following signs:

Alto	Halt
Cruzamento	Crossroads
Curva perigosa	Dangerous bend (curve)
Descida ingreme	Steep hill
Desvio	Diversion (detour)
Encruzilhada	Crossroads
Estacionamento permitido	Parking allowed

Lisbon

Estacionamento proíbido	No parking
Guiar com cuidado	Drive with care
Obras/Fim de obras	Road works (men working)/ end of road works
Paragem de autocarro	Bus stop
Pare	Stop
Passagem proíbida	No entry
Pedestres, peões	Pedestrians
Perigo	Danger
Posto de socorros	First-aid post
Proibida a entrada	No entry
Saída de camiões	Lorry (truck) exit
Seguir pela direita/esquerda	Keep right/left
Sem saída	No through road
Sentido proíbido	No entry
Sentido único	One-way street
Silêncio	Silence zone
Stop	Stop
Trabalhos	Road works (men working)
Trânsito proíbido	No through traffic
Veículos pesados	Heavy vehicles
Velocidade máxima	Maximum speed

Are we on the right road for …?	**É esta a estrada para …?**
Fill the tank, please, super.	**Encha o depósito de super, por favor.**
Check the oil/tyres/ battery, please.	**Verifique o óleo/os pneus/a bateria, se faz favor.**
I've broken down.	**O meu carro está avariado.**
There's been an accident.	**Houve um acidente.**

uid measures

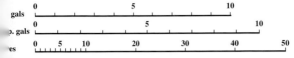

	0				5				10	
gals										
p. gals	0				5					10
es	0	5	10		20		30		40		50

istance

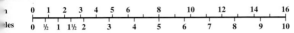

n	0	1	2	3	4	5	6		8		10		12		14		16
les	0	½	1	1½	2		3		4		5		6		7	8		9		10

E

LECTRIC CURRENT (*corrente eléctrica*)

tandard throughout Portugal is 220-volt, 50-cycle AC. For US appliances, transformers and plug adaptors are needed.

need an adaptor/a battery, lease.	**Preciso de um adaptador/uma pilha, por favor.**

MBASSIES and CONSULATES (*consulado; embaixada*)

Australia (Embassy): Avenida da Liberdade 244, 4°; tel. 52 33 50.

Canada (Embassy/Consulate): Avenida da Liberdade 144, 3°; el. 347 48 92.

Republic of Ireland (Embassy/Consulate): Rua da Imprensa à Estrela 1, 4°; tel. 396 15 69.

South Africa (Embassy): Avenida Luis Bivar 10/10 A; el. 53 50 41.

United Kingdom (Embassy): Rua de São Bernardo 33; tel. 396 11 91.

USA (Embassy/Consulate): Avenida das Forças Armadas 16; tel. 726 66 00.

Most embassies and consulates are open Mon-Fri from 9 or 10a
until 5pm, with a break in the middle of the day of 1-2¹/₂ hours.

Where's the British/American embassy?	**Onde é a embaixada inglesa/americana?**
It's very urgent.	**E muito urgente.**

EMERGENCIES (*urgência*) (See also MEDICAL CARE on p.118)
The following numbers are useful 24 hours a day in an emergency:

Police (and general emergency)	**115**
Fire	**342 22 22**, **60 60 60**
Ambulance (Red Cross)	**301 77 77**

The British Hospital (tel. 395 50 67) will help anyone in difficult
but there is no casualty department. Out-patients is open Mon-F
9am-8pm, and there is an on-call system for nights and weekends.

For emergency road service telephone the Road Patrol Police o
395 20 22. (See also DRIVING ON p.110)

Although you can call the police from any one of the blue boxes i
the street marked *polícia*, it's unlikely you'll get anyone on the othe
end who speaks anything but Portuguese.

For emergency dental care, the hospital of São José, Rua José An
tonio Serrano; tel. 886 01 31 or 887 31 31, has a 24-hour genera
emergency service which includes dental treatment.

ETIQUETTE (See also LANGUAGE on p.115)

A certain amount of formality seems inevitable in a country where
people tend to address strangers in the third person. 'How are you?'
and 'How is she/he?' are the same in Portuguese. However, although
the Portuguese tend to be reserved, they are extremely hospitable.

The Portuguese shake hands at every opportunity. Don't worry i
somebody taps you firmly on the arm to attract your attention, it's the
Portuguese way; nor if people, especially villagers, seem to be star-
ing at you – it's only unaffected curiosity.

G

AY and LESBIAN TRAVELLERS

a country heavily influenced by the Catholic Church, attitudes to-
ards gays are not as tolerant as elsewhere in Europe. Lisbon is the
ost important city in Portugal's gay scene and offers bars and clubs
hich cater to a gay crowd, including Bar 106, Rua de São Marcal
06 and Fragil, Rua da Atalaia 128. Also, on the Costa da Caparica,
n the west coast of the peninsula across the Tagus, beach no. 9 on
ne narrow-gauge railway is gay. As yet, there are no helplines.

UIDES and TOURS

All guides must belong to and meet the standards of the professional
ssociation of guides. A guide or interpreter can be hired directly
hrough their association in Lisbon at Rua do Telhal 4, 3°, tel. 346 71
70, 9am-1pm, 2.30-6pm.

Information on half- or full-day city tours is available from the
ourist office (see p.123) or travel agents.

We'd like an English-   **Queremos um guia que**
speaking guide.   **fale inglês.**

L

LANGUAGE

Portuguese, a derivative of Latin, is spoken in such far-flung spots as
Brazil and Macau. Your high-school Spanish may help with signs
and menus, but will not unlock the mysteries of spoken Portuguese.
Almost everyone understands Spanish and many speak French, having worked in France. Schoolchildren are taught French and English.

The Berlitz PORTUGUESE PHRASEBOOK AND DICTIONARY covers
most situations you're likely to encounter during a visit to Portugal.
Also useful is the Berlitz PORTUGUESE-ENGLISH/ENGLISH-POR-
TUGUESE POCKET DICTIONARY, containing a special menu-reader sup-
plement.

Lisbon

Here are some useful phrases to get you going (see also the front cover flap of this guide):

Good evening	**Boa noite**
Goodbye	**Adeus**
excuse me/you're welcome	**perdão/de nada**
where/when/how	**onde/quando/como**
yesterday/today/tomorrow	**ontem/hoje/amanhã**
day/week/month/year	**dia/semana/mês/ano**
left/right	**esquerdo/direito**
good/bad	**bom/mau**
big/small	**grande/pequeno**
cheap/expensive	**barato/caro**
hot/cold	**quente/frio**
old/new	**velho/novo**
open/closed	**aberto/fechado**
Please write it down.	**Escreva-mo, por favor.**
What does this mean?	**Que quer dizer isto?**
Help me, please.	**Ajude-me, por favor.**
Just a minute.	**Um momento.**
Get a doctor quickly.	**Chame um médico, depressa.**

DAYS

Sunday	**domingo**
Monday	**segunda-feira**
Tuesday	**terça-feira**
Wednesday	**quarta-feira**
Thursday	**quinta-feira**
Friday	**sexta-feira**
Saturday	**sábado**
What day is it today?	**Que dia é hoje?**

AUNDRY and DRY CLEANING (*lavandaria; tinturaria*)

There are self-service laundries in and around Lisbon; you can find
them listed under 'lavandarias e tinturarias' in the yellow pages
phone book. Their hours are limited (9am-1pm, 3-7pm weekdays,
9am-noon Saturday) and none are in the centre of Lisbon.

Most cleaners take three or four days, although one in the Rossio
station shopping centre will do urgent work for the next day.

When will it be ready?	**Quando estará pronto?**
I must have this for tomorrow morning.	**Preciso disto para amanhã de manhã.**

LOST PROPERTY (*objectos perdidos*)

The police have a special lost property office at Praça Cidade de Salazar Lote 180; tel. 853 85403. If you've lost something in a bus or
tram, go to the public transport lost-and-found department at the
base of the Santa Justa lift near the Rossio station; tel. 347 08 77.

I've lost my wallet/purse/passport.	**Perdi a minha carteira/mala/passaporte.**

M

MEDIA

Radio and TV (*rádio; televisão*). Four channels are widely available
in Portugal: two are government-run and two are independent. Films
are usually shown in the original language with subtitles.

The government operates four radio channels. Programme Two
consists of classical music, while Programme Four is mostly pop.
Travel suggestions in English are broadcast every morning on Programme Two (755 kHz medium wave, 94.3 MHz FM) at 8.15am.

The Voice of America, BBC, Radio Canada International and
other foreign stations can be picked up on short wave.

Newspapers and Magazines (*jornal; revista*). Europe's principal
newspapers, including most British dailies and the *International*

Lisbon

Herald Tribune, edited in Paris, are available on the day of publica-
tion at many newsagents and hotels. Popular foreign magazines ar
also sold at the same shops or stands. For cinema and theatre pro
grammes, check one of the local Portuguese-language dailies; th
most complete listings are in *Diário de Notícias*. The weekly *Se7e* (
play on the word for seven) has details of a wide range of events.

Have you any English-language newspapers?	**Tem jornais em inglês?**

MEDICAL CARE (See also EMERGENCIES on p.114)

Medical insurance to cover illness or accident while abroad is a good
investment. Your travel agent or insurance company can advise you
No vaccinations are required, but check first with your travel agent.

Farmácias (chemists/drugstores) are open during normal business
hours. At other times one shop in each neighbourhood is on duty
round the clock. Addresses are listed in newspapers.

a doctor	**um médico**
a dentist	**um dentista**
an ambulance	**uma ambulância**
hospital	**hospital**
an upset stomach	**mal de estômago**
sunstroke	**uma insolação**
a fever	**febre**

MONEY MATTERS

Currency (*moeda*). Don't worry if you see price tags quoting many
digits around a $ sign. Here it means *escudo* (abbreviated *esc*) and
the sign replaces the decimal point (thus 5,000$00 esc means 5,000
escudos). The escudo is divided into 100 *centavos*, although you
aren't likely to see centavo coins these days. Coins now in use are 1,
2½, 5, 10, 20, 50, 100 and 200 esc. Banknotes come in denomina-
tions of 500, 1,000 (equalling one *conto*), 5,000 and 10,000 esc.

Banks and Currency Exchange (*banco; câmbio*). Normal banking hours are Mon-Fri 8.30am-2.30/2.45pm. In tourist areas, some banks remain open later and at weekends to change money, and there is a 24-hour exchange office at the airport. The exchange office at Santa Apolónia railway station is open 8.30am-8.30pm and one bank in Praça dos Restauradores is open 6-11pm for the benefit of tourists. A substantial flat rate fee is charged for changing traveller's cheques, and you will need to show your passport. You can use the automatic teller machines outside many banks to get cash with a Visa or Mastercard credit card provided you know the personal identification number (PIN). Machines outside some banks in central Lisbon change certain foreign currency notes (bills), but not pounds sterling.

I want to change some pounds/dollars.	**Queria trocar libras/dólares.**
Can you cash a traveller's cheque?	**Pode pagar um cheque de viagem?**

Credit Cards (*cartão de crédito*). Standard international credit cards are accepted by most tourist establishments. In the hinterland, however, you may not be able to use a credit card. To cancel a credit card, contact UNICRE, the central clearing office; tel. 53 35 60.

Can I pay with this credit card?	**Posso pagar com cartão de crédito?**

Planning your budget. The following list will give some idea of prices in Portuguese escudos (esc). These should be regarded as approximate guidelines, however, as prices have been rising rapidly in Portugal in recent years.

Airport transfer. Bus to Cais do Sodré or Santa Apolónia station 175 esc, 'Linha verde' bus airport-Santa Apolónia station 470 esc. Taxi to Praça Marquês de Pombal 1,800 esc, to Cais do Sodré 2,000 esc (a surcharge must be paid if luggage exceeds 30kg/66lb).

Lisbon

Car rental (international company). *Opel Corsa 1000* (2 door) 4,200 esc per day plus 42 esc per km, or flat charge of 60,000 esc per week with no extra charge for distance travelled. *Ford Escort 1.3 L* (5 door) 6,300 esc per day plus 56 esc per km, or flat charge of 84,000 esc per week with no extra charge for distance travelled. Add 17% tax. **NB** Lower rates can be obtained by reserving in advance from outside the country. In some instances prices are almost halved.

Entertainment. Bullfight from 2,000 esc; cinema 600 esc; disco from 1,000 esc; *fado* from 5,000 esc.

Food and drink. Prices given are per person. Continental breakfast from 250 esc; lunch or dinner in good establishment from 2,500 esc; coffee from 70 esc, beer from 100 esc, Portuguese brandy from 100 esc, gin and tonic from 400 esc, bottle of house wine from 600 esc.

Guides. 10,000-12,000 esc per half day, 18,000-22,000 esc per day.

Hotels (double room with bath per night). 5-star 42,000 esc and over; 4-star 28,000 esc; 3-star 15,000 esc; 2-star 9,200 esc; 1-star 5,000 esc. Boarding house 4,000-6,000 esc.

Public transport. Metro 70 esc, 10 tickets for 500 esc; bus 175 esc, tram 175 esc, 10 tickets 1400 esc. Tourist pass for 4 days' unlimited travel on Lisbon's public transport system 1,500 esc, 7 days' 2,120 esc.

Taxi. Initial charge 250 esc. Praça Rossio to Gulbenkian Museum approx 450 esc; Praça Rossio to Belém approx 1,400 esc. Add 20% between 10pm and 8am.

OPENING HOURS (*horas de abertura*)

Most shops and offices open 9am-1pm and 3-7pm weekdays, and 9am-1pm Saturday. Museums are closed on Monday and public holidays, palaces on Monday or Tuesday. On every other day (including Sunday) they are open 10/11am-5pm, but most close noon-2pm or 1-

.30pm. A number of shopping centres scattered around Lisbon and
he suburbs open (10am-10pm), including Sunday.

P

PHOTOGRAPHY (*fotografia*) and VIDEO

Well-known brands of film in all sizes are sold at photo shops and
hotel news-stands. Colour film is processed in 2-3 days; shopping
centres and major supermarkets offer 1-hour processing facilities.

Airport security x-ray machines are safe for all but high speed
films, which should be passed across the counter for examination.
Standard and camcorder videotape is available. Note that European
pre-recorded tapes will not play on US equipment, and vice-versa.

I'd like a film for this camera.	**Quero um rolo para esta máquina.**
a black-and-white film	**um rolo a preto e branco**
a colour film	**um rolo a cores**
35mm film	**um rolo de trinta e cinco milímetros**
How long will it take to develop this film?	**Quanto tempo leva a revelar este filme?**
May I take a picture?	**Posso tirar uma fotografia?**

POLICE (*policia*) (See also EMERGENCIES on p.114)

The national police, wearing blue uniforms and armed with pistols,
maintain public order and oversee Lisbon traffic. They are generally
helpful and friendly and often speak a little English. Policemen as-
signed to traffic duty wear red armbands with a silver letter 'T' (for
Trânsito, or traffic) on a red background, a white helmet and white
gloves. On highways, traffic is controlled by the *Guarda Nacional
Republicana* (GNR) in white and red or white and blue cars, or on
motorcycles. Occasionally they make spot-checks on documents or
tyres. The way to address any policeman is '*Senhor Guarda*'.

Lisbon

Where's the nearest police station?

Onde fica o posto de polî/cia mais próximo?

PUBLIC HOLIDAYS (*feriado*)

1 January	*Ano Novo*	New Year's Day
25 April	*Dia da Liberdade*	Liberty Day
1 May	*Festa do Trabalho*	Labour Day
10 June	*Dia de Camões*	Camoens' Day
15 August	*Assunção*	Assumption
5 October	*Heróis da República*	Republic Day
1 November	*Todos-os-Santos*	All Saints' Day
1 December	*Dia da Independência*	Independence Day
8 December	*Imaculada Conceição*	Immaculate Conception
25 December	*Natal*	Christmas Day
Movable dates:	*Carnaval*	Shrove Tuesday /Carnival
	Sexta-feira Santa	Good Friday
	Corpo de Deus	Corpus Christi

These are only the national holidays of Portugal. Other special holidays affect different places and businesses. Lisbon, Estoril and Cascais have a local holiday on 13 June in honour of St Anthony (*Santo António*). Sintra has a holiday on 29 June (*São Pedro*).

Are you open tomorrow?

Estão abertos amanhã?

RELIGIOUS SERVICES

Most Portuguese are Roman Catholic. For English-speaking Catholics mass is held on Sunday at the Dominican Church of Corpo Santo, Travessa do Corpo Santo 32, Lisbon.

Anglican services are conducted in English on Sunday at St George's Church in the Estrêla district of Lisbon, west of the Bairro Alto, and at St Paul's, Avenida Bombeiros Voluntarios 1c, Estoril.

Church of Scotland (Presbyterian) services are held on the first
Sunday of every month at Rua da Arriaga 11; tel. 395 76 77.

The Shaare Tikva Synagogue is located at Rua Alexandre Herculano 59; tel. 388 15 92.

TIME DIFFERENCES

In 1992 Portugal switched time zones to align it with most of the European Union. Now it is at GMT + 1 in winter, making sunrise rather
late. From the first Sunday in April to the first Sunday in October the
clocks are moved one hour ahead for summer time, GMT + 2. In
summer the chart looks like this:

New York	London	Paris	**Lisbon**	Sydney	Auckland
6am	11am	noon	**noon**	8pm	10pm

TIPPING

Hotel and restaurant bills are generally all-inclusive, but feel free to
give a tip if the service is good. The following are just suggestions.

Hairdresser/barber	10%
Hotel maid, per week	500 esc
Lavatory attendant	25-50 esc
Hotel porter, per bag	100 esc
Taxi driver	10%
Tour guide	10-15% of excursion fare
Waiter	5-10%

TOURIST INFORMATION OFFICES

Canada: Suite 1005, 60 Bloor Street West, Toronto, Ont. M4W 3B8;
tel. (416) 921 7376.

Japan: Regency Shinsaka 101, 8-5-8 Akasaka, Minato-ku, Tokyo
107; tel. (3) 5474 4400.

United Kingdom: 22/25a Sackville St, London W1X 1DE; tel.
(071)494 1441.

Lisbon

USA: 590 Fifth Ave, New York 10036; tel. (212) 354 4403.

In Lisbon, the national tourist office (*Direcção-Geral do Turismo*) is located at Avenida António Augusto de Aguiar 86, 1000 Lisboa; tel 315 50 91. More convenient to the city centre is the information office in Palácio Foz, on Praça dos Restauradores; tel. 346 36 43.

The Lisbon tourist office (*Posto de Turismo da Camara Municipal de Lisboa*) is at the Amoreiras shopping centre; tel. 65 74 86. Dial 70 63 41 for information in English, but this line can be very busy.

TRANSPORT

Local buses. Bus stops have signs indicating the numbers of buses which stop there, and many give details of their routes. You can get a free map of the entire transit system at information posts of Carris (literally 'rails'), the local transport authority. The main one is at the base of the Santa Justa lift, near the Rossio station, where you can also buy economical passes and tickets in advance. Most buses load from the front: you pay the driver or show him your pre-paid ticket before putting it in the clipping machine. Others load from the rear – just follow the crowd.

Inter-city buses. Lisbon's bus terminals serve different parts of the country. Ask where the bus leaves from at the tourist office in Praça dos Restauradores. Buses are good and prices are reasonable.

Two sample journeys: Express buses from Lisbon to Castelo Branco, 256km (160 miles), take about 4 hours, and from Lisbon to Coimbra, 200km (125 miles), 3½ hours. On routes such as Lisbon-Sesimbra and Lisbon-Nazaré, there are only slower, local buses.

Trams. Tram stops are indicated by large signs marked Paragem (stop). The Carris bus map shows tram routes as well. Most trams are entered at the front, where you buy a ticket from the driver. On funiculars you pay at the door.

Metro. Lisbon's underground railway system, the Metropolitano, or Metro, has only 20 stations, most in residential districts. The entry points are not always clearly marked – the 'M' sign may be obscure or missing. Charts of the system are displayed in every station and carriage. Directions in several languages are posted in the stations.

Trains (*comboio*). Lisbon has four principal railway stations. International services and trains for northern Portugal leave from Santa Apolónia station, reached by bus 9 or 9a from Avenida da Liberdade. Commuter trains for the western suburbs and Estoril and Cascais leave from Cais do Sodré, while trains for Sintra and the west depart from Rossio station. The fourth station, called Sul e Sueste (South and South-east), has ferryboats which cross the Tagus to connect with trains to the Algarve. The ticket price includes the ferry link (See also Ferries below).

In the major stations, first- and second-class tickets are sold at separate windows. A first-class carriage usually has a yellow stripe above the windows and the number '1' near the doors.

Taxis (táxi). Lisbon taxis are beige, or black with a green roof, and have a sign reading taxi. In rural areas cars marked 'A' (meaning aluguer – for hire) operate as taxis, but without meters. Every neighbourhood has a taxi rank, as do most railway, Metro and ferry stations.

The fare is shown on the meter. Check that it's running; if not, the 'bill' might reflect it. Drivers add 20% at night and extra if you have more than 30kg (66lb) of baggage. A tip of 10% is appropriate.

Ferries. The two main ferry stations are next to each other: the **Sul e Sueste** (the larger building) and the **Alfândega** quay. The first serves only Seixal and Barreiro, from where south-bound trains depart (See also Trains above).

From the Alfândega quay, ferries run to Cacilhas/Almada and Montijo. You can also catch the Cacilhas/Almada ferry at the Cais do Sodré ferry station near the railway station of the same name.

From July to September, there are four ferry crossings a day between Sesimbra, Setúbal and the peninsula of Tróia. Frequent hovercraft services connect Tróia and Setúbal.

Lisbon

Tickets: You can buy tourist passes (*passe para turistas*) valid for 4 or 7 days on the Metro, trams, buses and funiculars within the main transport zone of Lisbon. There is also a book of ten tickets (*caderneta*) available for the Metro at the ticket window.

Hitch-hiking: Apart from on motorways (expressways), where it is forbidden, hitch-hiking should pose no big problems. As everywhere, women are advised not to hitch-hike alone.

How much is a ticket to …?	**Quanto custa o bilhete para …?**
Will you tell me when to get off?	**Pode dizer-me quando devo descer?**
Where's the nearest bus/tram stop?	**Onde fica a mais próxima paragem dos autocarros /eléctricos?**
Where can I get a taxi?	**Onde posso encontrar um táxi?**
What's the fare to …?	**Quanto custa o percurso até …?**
Can you give us a lift to …?	**Pode levar-nos a …?**

TRAVELLERS WITH DISABILITIES

Lisbon is not an easy city to negotiate; hills are steep and much of the road surface poor. In addition, the public transport system is not modern enough to consider the needs of disabled travellers.

The National Rehabilitation Secretariat, Avenida Conde Valbom 63, 1000 Lisbon, publishes a guide to transport facilities (in Portuguese) and an *Access Guide to Lisbon*. The Portuguese National Tourist Office provides a list of hotels suitable for wheelchair users.

Before you go, contact the Holiday Care Service, who are experts in the field of holidays for disabled people and will try to answer specific enquiries; tel (0293) 774535.

TRAVELLING TO LISBON

By Air

From the UK and Ireland: Lisbon is a very popular package tour destination, using charter flights and scheduled services, with either all-inclusive or self-catering holidays as well as fly/drive and flight-only arrangements. Ask your travel agent for more details.

From North America: Tours are available to Lisbon in combination with other Iberian or European destinations. For tours to Portugal only, you can either make independent air, transfer and hotel (plus car rental) arrangements, or book a fly/drive package.

By Car

The main access road to Lisbon from France is through Spain at the western end of the Pyrenees. A motorway (expressway) runs from Biarritz (France) to Burgos. From there, take either the N1 to Madrid and continue on E4 via Badajoz and Setúbal to Lisbon, or the N620 and then the E3 via Valladolid, Salamanca, Guarda and Coimbra. Driving distances from the UK are reduced by taking a long-distance car ferry to northern Spain: Plymouth or Portsmouth to Santander, and Portsmouth to Bilbao. Drivers from the UK can use the Le Shuttle Channel Tunnel service, which crosses from Dover to Calais in about 35 minutes.

By Rail

There are two main routes to Lisbon via Paris (a journey of about 24 hours): to Hendaye (south-west France) via Fuentes de Onoro/Vilar Formoso (Spanish/Portuguese frontier points); or via Madrid and Valencia de Alcántara (frontier point). From the UK, both routes offer a choice of sea crossings.

Inter-Rail and Rail Europ Senior tickets are valid in Portugal, as is the Eurailpass for non-European residents (sign before you leave)

WATER

Although Lisbon's tap water tastes heavily of chemicals, it's safe to drink. If you prefer bottled water, there is also an excellent range of local mineral waters.

a bottle of mineral water	**uma garrafa de água mineral**
carbonated/non-carbonated	**com/sem gás**

Lisbon

WEIGHTS and MEASURES (For fuel and distance charts see
DRIVING on p.110)

Length

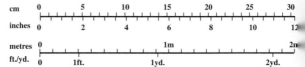

Weight

Temperature

WOMEN TRAVELLERS

Despite the Latino temperament, Portugal is a relatively safe country
for women travellers, but in the main cities of Lisbon and Oporto and
along the Algarve coast you should take care. Try to avoid bus and
train stations at night, and in Lisbon don't stray too far off the beaten
track, especially around the Bairro Alto.

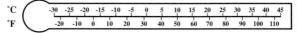

YOUTH HOSTELS (*pousadas de juventude*)

Young visitors of 14 years and over can stay in dormitories at very
low rates if they are members of a national or international youth
hostel association. Membership of the Portuguese Youth Hostel Association is open to 'juniors' (aged 14-21) and 'seniors' (22-40). Par-
ents with children younger than 14 may stay in these hostels if there
is room. Contact the Associação Portuguesa de Pousadas de Juven-
tude at Avenida Duque de Ávila 137, 1000 Lisbon; tel. 355 90 81.

A SELECTION OF HOTELS AND RESTAURANTS

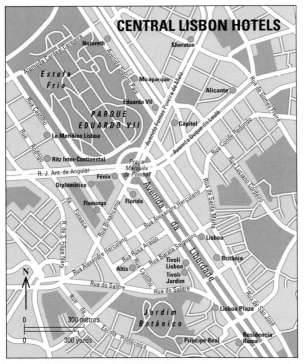

CENTRAL LISBON HOTELS

Nazareth
Sheraton
Alameda Cardeal Cerejeira
Estufa Fria
Avenida Sidónio Pais
Miraparque
Alicante
Rua de Tomás Fiemo
Rua Castilho
Eduardo VII
PARQUE EDUARDO VII
Le Meridien Lisboa
Capitol
Avenida Fontes Pereira de Melo
Avenida Duque de Loulé
Rua Conde Redondo
Ritz Inter-Continental
R. J. Ant. de Anguiar
Praça Marquês de Pombal
Rua Luciano Cordeiro
Fénix
Diplomático
Rua de Santa Marta
Flamingo
Florida
Avenida da Liberdade
Rua Alexandre Herculano
Rua Braancamp
da Fonseca
R. de S. Filipe Ney
Rua Alexandre Herculano
Rua Rosa Araujo
Lisboa
Rua Barata Salgueiro
Altis
Rua Castilho
Tivoli Lisboa
Britânia
Tivoli Jardim
Rua de São José
Rua do Salitre
Rua do Salitre
N
Lisboa Plaza
Jardim Botânico
0   300 metres
0   300 yards
Escola Politécnica
Príncipe Real
Residencia Roma

Recommended Hotels

Hotel prices have risen in recent years to match most western European destinations, but even the most luxurious places offer special packages (such as summer or weekend reductions at hotels which normally rely on corporate business). It's always worth asking.

The hotels below are listed by geographical location and alphabetical order, and cover the excursion areas in this guide as well as Lisbon itself. Central Lisbon covers the area from the waterfront up to Praça Marquês de Pombal (many hotels are in the vicinity of the traffic circle); North Lisbon refers to the area beyond Praça Marquês de Pombal. Where possible, fax as well as telephone numbers have been listed.

The price indication given is for a double room, with breakfast, including service and VAT (currently 5% of room price).

✪✪✪✪	over 35,000 esc
✪✪✪	20,000 to 35,000 esc
✪✪	12,000 to 20,000 esc
✪	below 12,000 esc

CENTRAL LISBON

Altis ✪✪✪ *Rua Castilho 11, 1200 Lisbon; Tel. 52 24 96; fax 54 86 96.* 307 rooms. A large and luxurious hotel with all the modern standard comforts. Some of the facilities include an indoor swimming pool, sauna and health club. Enjoy the delicious food served in the rooftop restaurant, which offers lovely views over the city.

Americano ✪ *Rua 1° de Dezembro 73, 1200 Lisbon; Tel. 347 49 76.* 50 rooms. Conveniently located in the busy heart of the city, close to the Praça Rossio. No restaurant.

Capitol ✪✪ *Rua Eça de Queiroz 24, 1000 Lisbon; Tel. 353 68 11; fax 352 61 65.* 58 rooms. Comfortable hotel in a side street near Edward VII Park.

Da Lapa ✪✪✪✪ *Rua do Pau de Bandeira, 1200 Lisbon; Tel. 395 00 05; fax 395 06 65.* 102 rooms. In the Lapa district, a luxurious conversion of a palatial old mansion overlooking the River Tagus. Indoor and outdoor swimming pools and magnificent landscaped gardens.

Eduardo VII ✪✪✪ *Avenida Fontes Pereira de Melo 5, 1000 Lisbon; Tel. 353 01 41; fax 53 38 79.* 121 rooms. This is a stylish, older style hotel, and close to the splendid park of the same name. Great views over the park from the rooftop restaurant and terrace.

Fénix ✪✪✪ *Praça Marquês de Pombal 8, 1200 Lisbon; Tel. 386 21 21; fax 386 01 31.* 122 rooms. A comfortable, recently renovated older hotel with a good restaurant serving traditional regional dishes.

Insulana ✪ *Rua da Assunção 52-2°, 1100 Lisbon; Tel. 342 76 25.* 32 rooms. Simple and small, but very comfortable, this economy hotel is situated right in the heart of the downtown Baixa district. No restaurant.

Lisboa ✪✪✪ *Rua Barata Salgueiro 5, 1100 Lisbon; Tel. 355 41 31; fax 355 41 39.* 61 rooms. A hotel with all the standard modern comforts, including air-conditioning and satellite television. No restaurant.

Lisboa Plaza ✪✪✪ *Travessa do Salitre 7, 1200 Lisbon; Tel. 346 39 22; fax 347 16 30.* 112 rooms. Stylish, recently renovated hotel, in a central location near Avenida da Liberdade. A noted restaurant serving the usual Portuguese specialities.

Lisboa-Tejo ✪✪ *Poço do Borratéém 4, 1100 Lisbon; Tel. 886 51 63; fax 886 51 63.* 60 rooms. 19th-century hotel near Rossio, completely refurbished with modern facilities.

Lisbon

Le Meridien Lisboa ✪✪✪✪ *Rua Castilho 149, 1000 Lisbon; Tel. 69 09 00; fax 69 32 31.* 331 rooms. Bright, modern luxury hotel next to Edward VII Park, with a health club and sauna.

Miraparque ✪✪ *Avenida Sidónio Pais 12, 1000 Lisbon; Tel. 352 42 86; fax 57 89 20.* 100 rooms. An old-style building with compact, modern rooms facing Edward VII Park.

Mundial ✪✪✪ *Rua Dom Duarte 4, 1100 Lisbon; Tel. 886 31 01; fax 887 91 29.* 147 rooms. Cylindrical 10-storey block in busy central area, with a rooftop restaurant offering views of the old city.

Nazareth ✪ *Avenida António Augusto de Aguiar 25, 1000 Lisbon; Tel. 54 20 16; Fax 356 08 36.* 32 rooms. Economical hotel in a central location, close to Edward VII Park. No restaurant.

Principe Real ✪✪✪ *Rua da Alegria 53, 1200 Lisbon; Tel. 346 01 16; Fax 342 21 04.* 24 rooms. Pleasant small hotel, rather like a private club, and in a good central location between the Botanic Gardens and Avenida da Liberdade.

Residencial Nova Silva ✪✪ *Rua Victor Gordon 11, Lisbon; Tel. 342 43 71.* Small but functional rooms in this charming pensione near Praça do Comércio. Very warm, friendly atmosphere and lovely views over the River Tagus.

Residencial Roma ✪ *Travessa da Glória 22A-1°, 1200 Lisbon; Tel. 346 05 57; fax 346 05 57 .* 24 rooms. Friendly and economical, this hotel is in a great central location, near to Praça dos Restauradores. No restaurant.

Tivoli Jardim ✪✪✪ *Rua Julio Cesar Machado 7, 1200 Lisbon; Tel. 353 99 71; fax 355 65 66.* 119 rooms. Near Praça Marquês de Pombal, with a lovely, heated outdoor swimming pool and tennis facilities.

Tivoli Lisboa ✪✪✪ *Avenida da Liberdade 185, 1200 Lisbon; Tel. 356 13 00; fax 57 94 61.* 327 rooms. Facilities include a noted rooftop restaurant, a heated outdoor swimming pool and tennis courts. Outdoor dining is a must in the summer.

York House ✪✪✪ *Rua das Janelas Verdes 32, 1200 Lisbon; Tel. 396 24 35; fax 397 27 93.* 35 rooms. Near the Museum of Ancient Art, west of the centre in a converted 16th century convent overlooking the River Tagus. Outdoor dining in the garden courtyard during the summer.

NORTH LISBON

Albergaria Pax ✪ *Rua José Estêvão 20, 1100 Lisbon; Tel. 356 81 61; fax 315 57 55.* 34 rooms in a small, but pleasant hotel. No restaurant.

Alfa Lisboa ✪✪✪ *Avenida Columbano Bordalo Pinheiro, 1000 Lisbon; Tel. 726 27 28; fax 726 30 31.* 350 rooms. Modern tower block north west of the city centre, providing all modern comforts. Business oriented, stylish and with good views.

Dom João ✪ *Rua José Estêvão 43, 1100 Lisbon; Tel. 52 41 71; fax 352 45 69.* 18 rooms in this friendly economy hotel. No restaurant.

Dom Manuel I ✪✪ *Avenida Duque d'Avila 189, 1000 Lisbon; Tel. 356 14 10; fax 57 69 85.* 64 rooms. Situated in a quiet area close to the Gulbenkian Museum, with relatively large rooms and pleasant decor. No restaurant.

Holiday Inn Crowne Plaza ✪✪✪✪ *Avenida Marechal Craveiro, Lopes 390, 1700 Lisbon; Tel. 759 96 39; fax 758 66 05.* 221 rooms. A modern block in the Campo Grande area and conveniently close to the airport.

Lisboa Penta ✪✪✪ *Avenida dos Combatentes, 1600 Lisbon; Tel. 726 46 29; fax 726 42 81.* 588 rooms. Large, business oriented hotel near the Gulbenkian Museum. Garden, outdoor swimming pool, health club and sauna. Shuttle bus to the city centre.

Lisbon

Lutécia ✪✪✪ *Avenida Frei Miguel, Contreiras 52, 1700 Lisbon; Tel. 80 31 21; fax 80 78 18.* 150 rooms. A modern hotel block between the city centre and airport. Great views of north Lisbon.

Novotel Lisboa ✪✪ *Avenida José Malhoa 1642, 1000 Lisbon; Tel. 726 60 22; fax 726 64 96.* 246 rooms. Modern block with an outdoor swimming pool and good views of Campo Grande, the aqueduct and Monsanto Park.

Principe ✪✪ *Avenida Duque d'Avila 201, 1000 Lisbon; Tel. 353 61 51; fax 353 43 14.* 68 rooms. Comfortable hotel situated in a great location between the city centre and airport.

Roma ✪✪ *Avenida de Roma 33, 1700 Lisbon; Tel. 796 77 61; fax 793 29 81.* 265 rooms. Informal hotel, very convenient for the airport and with views of north Lisbon. Rooftop restaurant, indoor swimming pool and sauna.

Sheraton Lisboa and Towers ✪✪✪✪ *Rua Latinho Coelho 1, 1097 Lisbon; Tel. 57 57 57; fax 54 71 64.* 384 rooms. Modern tower block, east of Edward VII Park, and with a lively atmosphere. Heated outdoor swimming pool and health club and sauna.

ESTORIL COAST

Albatroz ✪✪✪✪ *Rua Frederico Arouca 100, 2750 Cascais; Tel. (01) 483 28 21; Fax (01) 284 48 27.* 40 rooms. Elegant mansion, extended to create an exclusive luxury retreat high above the Praia da Rainha beach. Outdoor pool and lovely gardens.

Casa da Pergola ✪✪ *Aveinda Valbom 13, 2750 Cascais; Tel. (01) 484 00 40.* 10 rooms. A beautifully furnished guest house just a couple of blocks away from the beach. Closed from November-March.

Central ✪✪ *Praça da Republica, Sintra; Tel. (01) 923 09 63.* 14 rooms. Small but comfortable, old-fashioned hotel right opposite the Palácio Nacional.

Recommended Hotels

Cidadela ✪✪✪ *Avenida 25 de Abril, 2750 Cascais; Tel. (01) 483 29 21; Fax (01) 483 72 26.* 130 rooms. Located in a residential area just a few blocks away from the beach, this is a modern resort hotel with good facilities, including an outdoor swimming pool and gardens.

Estalagem Fundador ✪✪ *Rua Dom Afonso Henriques 161, 2765 Estoril; Tel. (01) 468 23 46; Fax (01) 468 87 79.* 10 rooms. A small but very pleasant guest house above a park, with an outdoor swimming pool.

Estoril Sol ✪✪✪ *Parque Palmela, 2750 Cascais; Tel. (01) 483 2831; Fax (01) 483 22 80.* 317 rooms. Towering high over the bay of Cascais, this is a luxurious resort hotel in a great location close to the beach. Freshwater and seawater pools, squash courts and sauna are just a few of the sports facilities available.

Lido ✪✪ *Rua do Alentejo 12, 2765 Estoril; Tel. (01) 468 4098; Fax (01) 268 36 65.* 60 rooms. A pleasant modern holiday hotel situated in a peaceful area some distance from the sea. Lovely well-tended garden and swimming pool.

Palácio ✪✪✪ *Rua do Parque, 2765 Estoril; Tel. (01) 468 04 00; Fax (01) 468 4867.* 162 rooms. Long-established luxury grand hotel, which looks like a cruise ship and is as palatial as its name suggests. Heated outdoor pool, tennis and gardens. Special rates for guests at its golf course.

Palacio de Seteais ✪✪✪✪ *Rua Barbosa do Bocage, 2710 Sintra; Tel. (01) 923 32 00; Fax (01) 923 42 77* 30 rooms. A luxury hotel in an historic and beautiful 18th-century palace. Antique furniture, gardens, and superb views of the Castelo dos Mouros, Pena Palace and the surrounding countryside. Sports facilities include tennis courts and a heated outdoor pool.

Quinta da Capela ✪✪ *Estrada de Monserrate, 2710 Sintra; Tel. (01) 929 34 05; Fax (01) 929 34 25.* Eleven attractive rooms in a beautiful, rambling 16th-century house on an old country estate, around 3km (2 miles) from Sintra. No restaurant. Closed from November-February.

SOUTH OF LISBON

Albergaria Solaris ✪ *Praça Marquês de Pombal 12, 2900 Setúbal; Tel. (065) 52 21 89; Fax (065) 52 20 70.* 24 rooms. Fine old house on a quiet square, with well-equipped, modernized rooms. No restaurant.

Esperença ✪ *Avenida Luisa Todi 220, 2900 Setúbal; Tel. (065) 52 51 51; fax (065) 302 83.* 76 rooms. Near the historic centre of town, a simple but comfortable modern block; business oriented.

Hotel do Mar ✪✪✪ *Rua General Humberto Delgado, 2970 Sesimbra; Tel. (01) 223 33 26; Fax (01) 223 38 88.* 168 rooms. A modern holiday hotel with great sea views, beautiful gardens, indoor and outdoor pools and tennis courts.

Ibis ✪ *Vale da Rosa, 2900 Setúbal; Tel. (065) 77 22 00; fax (065) 77 24 47.* 102 rooms. Comfortable, modern and economical accommodation about 5km (3 miles) south of the port. Outdoor pool.

Pousada de Palmela ✪✪✪ *Castelo de Palmela, 2950 Palmela; Tel. (01) 235 12 26; Fax (01) 233 04 40.* 28 rooms. A luxury *pousada* built in a hilltop fortress-monastery overlooking Setúbal and the sea. Notable restaurant serving local dishes, especially seafood.

Pousada de São Filipe ✪✪✪ *Castelo de São Filipe, 2900 Setúbal; Tel. (065) 52 38 44; Fax (065) 53 25 38.* 14 rooms. A luxury *pousada* inside the walls of a fortress built in 1590, just west of the port of Setúbul. Some rooms are in the former castle's dungeons. Quite close to the Serra de Arrábida National Park.

Quinta do César ✪✪ *Vila Fresca de Azeitão, 2925 Azeitão, Setúbal; Tel. (01) 208 03 87; no fax.* Four rooms in a delightful, large country mansion in a beautiful hilltop town. The spacious public areas are complemented by the lovely gardens and the outdoor swimming pool.

Residencial Espadarte ✪ *Avenida 25 de Abril, 2970 Sesimbra; Tel. (01) 223 31 89; Fax (01) 223 32 94.* 80 rooms. Modern, functional holiday accommodation, right on the seafront. No restaurant.

TO THE NORTH

Albergaria Josefa D'Óbidos ✪ *Rua Dom João de Ornelas, 2510 Óbidos; Tel. (062) 95 92 28; Fax (062) 95 95 33.* 38 rooms. Newly built in the traditional Portuguese style, just outside the walls near the main gate. Named after the renowned 17th-century artist, with reproductions of some of her best works displayed on the walls.

Casa da Pedeira ✪✪ *Estrada N8, Aljubarrota, 2460 Alcobaça; Tel. (062) 50 82 72; Fax (062) 50 82 72.* 12 rooms. A family-run inn with that personal touch, situated just 6km (4 miles) from Alcobaça in the direction of Batalha. No formal restaurant, but dinner is available if prior notice is given.

Estalagem Dom Gonçalo ✪ *Rua Jacinta Marto 100, 2495 Fátima; Tel. (049) 53 30 62; Fax (049) 53 20 88.* 45 rooms. Very close to the Sanctuary in the centre of town, this is a simple but pleasant modern building with well-equipped rooms.

Hotel da Nazaré ✪✪ *Largo Afonso Zuquete 7, 2450 Nazaré; Tel. (062) 56 13 11; Fax (062) 56 12 38.* 52 rooms. A well established holiday hotel in the town, just a short walk from the beach.

Hotel da Praia Norte ✪✪ *Praia Norte, 2520 Peniche; Tel. (062) 78 11 66; Fax (062) 78 11 65.* 92 rooms. A modern holiday hotel near the sandy beach, offering an outdoor pool and tennis facilities.

Hotel de Fátima ✪ *Rua João Paulo II, 2496 Fátima; Tel. (049) 53 33 51; Fax (049) 53 26 91.* 133 rooms. A modern, plain but comfortable hotel, in a handy central location near the Sanctuary.

Pedro o Pescador ✪ *Rua Dr Eduardo Burnay 22, 2655 Ericeira; Tel. (061) 86 43 02; Fax (061) 623 21.* 25 rooms. A friendly and informal holiday hotel, only a short walk from the beach. Closed throughout January.

Pensão Ribamar ✪ *Rua Gomes Freire 9, 2450 Nazaré; Tel. (062) 55 11 58.* 23 rooms. A plain but comfortable traditional boarding house near the beach with a relaxed and friendly atmosphere.

Pousada do Castelo ✪✪✪ *2510 Óbidos; Tel. (062) 95 91 05; Fax (062) 95 91 48.* 9 rooms. This is a luxurious pousada in part of the medieval castle, inside the walled town. Celebrated restaurant serving regional and national dishes.

Pousada do Mestre Afonso Domingues ✪✪ *2440 Batalha; Tel. (044) 96 260; Fax (044) 96 247.* 21 rooms. Named after the architect of the great monastery opposite, this is a new and comfortable pousada with spacious and attractive public rooms and an excellent restaurant serving regional specialities such as roast leg of pork.

Quinta do Campo ✪✪ *Valado dos Frades, 2450 Nazaré; Tel. (062) 57 71 35; Fax (062) 57 75 55.* 8 rooms. Family-run accommodation in this charming old manor house, once part of an old monastic estate, just 5km (3 miles) from Nazaré on the road to Alcobaça. Swimming pool, tennis and beautiful gardens. Dinner is available if prior notice is given.

Quinta do Fidalgo ✪✪ *2440 Batalha; Tel. (044) 96114; Fax (044) 96114.* Five charming rooms in a family run manor house with attractive gardens opposite the monastery.

Vilazul ✪ *Calçada de Baleia 10, 2655 Ericeira; Tel. (061) 86 41 01; Fax (061) 62 927.* 21 rooms. A well converted, pleasant old house in the town centre, with a lovely rooftop lounge and bar. Restaurant serves noted Portuguese and international dishes.

Recommended Restaurants

There's no shortage of good places to eat in Lisbon, and they cater for all tastes and pockets, offering everything from cheap snack bars and coffee bars to elegant dining rooms hung with chandeliers.

Everything costs less away from the 'tourist areas'. Paradoxically, though, the 'tourist menu' in many restaurants, especially at lunchtime, can be excellent value at 1,500-2,500 esc, with either wine, beer, mineral water or a soft drink included.

The prices indicated are for starter, main course and dessert, per person. Some fish or shell-fish dishes may be more expensive. Service and VAT of 16% are included – as they generally are in the bill.

✪✪✪	over 6000 esc
✪✪	4,000-6000 esc
✪	below 4,000 esc

BAIRRO ALTO

Adega Machado ✪✪✪ *Rua do Norte 91, 1200 Lisbon; Tel. 342 87 13.* Very popular with visitors from abroad. Dinner only, with traditional *fado* and other folk music. Closed Monday.

Arcadas do Faia ✪✪✪ *Rua da Barroca 56, 1200 Lisbon; Tel. 342 67 42.* Serves traditional Portuguese cuisine with the accompaniment of *fado* and other folk music. Dinner only. Closed Sunday.

Bachus ✪✪ *Largo da Trindade 9, 1200 Lisbon; Tel. 342 28 28.* An attractive and very fashionable restaurant serving fine dishes from regions of Portugal and international cuisine. Closed Sunday.

Bota Alta ✪✪ *Travessa da Queimada 37, 1200 Lisbon; Tel. 32 79 59.* Down to earth and friendly local bistro with bright, fun decor and cheerful staff. Very busy most evenings – you will probably have to wait for a table. Portuguese fare and wholesome old favourites.

Brasuca ✪ *Rua João Pereira da Rosa 7, 1200 Lisbon; Tel. 342 85 42.* This is an informal restaurant specializing in a variety of traditional Brazilian and Portuguese dishes. A good selection of wholesome food is served in a relaxed atmosphere. Closed Monday.

Casa Faz Frio ✪ *Rua de Dom Pedro V 96, 1200 Lisbon; Tel. 346 18 60.* All the goodness of traditional Portuguese food served in a lovely tiled restaurant which looks like an old, country wine cellar.

Cervejeria da Trindade ✪ *Rua Nova da Trindade 20, 1200 Lisbon; Tel. 342 35 06.* Big beer hall and restaurant decorated with azulejo-covered walls. Portuguese cooking and seafood specialities at good prices.

Conventual ✪✪ *Praça das Flores 45, 1200 Lisbon; Tel. 60 91 96.* Just west of the busy Bairro Alto, this restaurant serves fine Portuguese cuisine. Closed Saturday lunchtime, Sunday and August.

O Forcado ✪✪✪ *Rua da Rosa 221, 1200 Lisbon; Tel. 346 85 79.* Traditional folk music is a charming accompaniment to the variety of Portuguese and international dishes on offer here. Open in the evenings only. Closed Wednesday.

Mamma Rosa ✪ *Rua do Grémio Lusitano, 1200 Lisbon; Tel. 346 53 50.* An informal restaurant with an Italian theme, serving pizzas and other well-known Italian dishes. Evenings only. Closed Sunday.

Pap d'Açorda ✪✪ *Rua da Atalaia 57, 1200 Lisbon; Tel. 346 48 11.* Traditional Portuguese food with the noted açorda (shellfish stew) as the main speciality. Closed Sunday and Monday.

Porta Branca ✪✪ *Rua do Teixeira 35, 1200 Lisbon; Tel. 342 10 24.* Well known for mouth-watering steaks, but also serving a variety of Portuguese seafood and regional dishes. Closed Saturday lunchtime, Sunday and July.

A Quinta ✪ *Passarela do Elevador de Santa Justa, 1200 Lisbon, Tel. 346 55 88.* At the top of the elevator and affording good views over the Baixa district; this establishment is famous for both good international and local cooking. Closed Sunday.

A Severa ✪✪✪ *Rua das Gáveas 51, 1200 Lisbon; Tel. 342 83 14.* Enjoy traditional Portuguese food to the accompaniment of the fado lament and other folk music in the evening. Closed Thursday.

Tavares ✪✪✪ *Rua da Misericórdia 37, 1200 Lisbon; Tel. 342 11 12.* A stylish restaurant, serving classical French cuisine. Closed Saturday and public holidays.

CENTRAL LISBON

Aviz ✪✪✪ *Rua Serpa Pinto 12-B, 1200 Lisbon; Tel. 342 83 91.* This is a stylish restaurant in the Baixa district offering fine Portuguese and French cuisine. Closed Saturday lunchtime, Sunday and throughout August.

Bom Jardim – Rei dos Frangos ✪ *Travessa de Santo Antão 11, 1200 Lisbon; Tel. 32 43 89.* A busy and informal place specializing in grills.

Casa da Comida ✪✪✪ *Travessa das Amoreiras 1, 1200 Lisbon; Tel. 388 53 76.* Pleasant patio setting in an old mansion near the aqueduct. Portuguese and French cuisine served outdoors. Closed Saturday lunch, Sunday and August.

Chester ✪✪✪ *Rua Rodrigo da Fonseca 87-D, 1200 Lisbon; Tel. 388 78 11.* Meat specialities are served in this restaurant, near Praça Marquês de Pombal (Rotunda). Closed Sunday and public holidays.

Lisbon

Gambrinus ✪✪✪ *Rua das Portas de Santo Antão 25, 1100 Lisbon; Tel. 342 14 66.* Choose from the great variety of traditional Portuguese dishes. This restaurant is expensive, but noted for its fresh seafood specialities cooked in different regional styles.

Pabe ✪✪✪ *Rua Duque de Palmela 27-A, 1200 Lisbon; Tel. 53 74 84.* Situated near the Praça Marquês de Pombal (Rotunda), this cosy, English-style pub is well known for serving international and Portuguese cuisine.

Restaurante 33 ✪✪ *Rua Alexandre Herculano 33A, 1200 Lisbon; Tel. 54 60 79.* Enjoy a typical Portuguese meal charmingly accompanied by folk music. Closed Saturday lunchtime and Sunday.

Ribadouro ✪✪ *Avenida da Liberdade 155, 1200 Lisbon; Tel. 54 94 11.* For a more informal meal, try this relaxed basement bar and restaurant which specializes in seafood.

São Caetano ✪✪✪ *Rua de São Caetano 27/31, 1200 Lisbon; Tel. 397 47 92.* An elegant restaurant in the Lapa district. One of the great attractions is the nightly fado entertainment which usually accompanies the meals. Dinner only. Closed Saturday lunchtime and Sunday.

Senhor Vinho ✪✪✪ *Rua do Meio à Lapa 18, 1200 Lisbon; Tel. 397 26 81.* This restaurant in the Lapa district, notable for serving traditional Portuguese food, is open for dinner only. Enjoy a relaxing meal while listening to the melancholy tunes of the fado and other entertainment. Closed Sunday.

Solmar ✪✪-✪✪✪ *Rua Portas de São Antão 108, 1200 Lisbon; Tel. 342 33 71.* A large and busy, informal restaurant in the heart of the busy Baixa district. It specializes in fresh fish and offers a wide variety of seafood dishes; shellfish is expensive.

Tágide ✪✪✪ *Largo da Academia Nacional de Belas Artes 18, 1200 Lisbon; Tel. 342 07 20.* This restaurant is situated west of the Praça do Comércio in an elegant, old house offering magnificent views of the waterfront, cathedral and square. Sample just a few of the excellent international and traditional Portuguese dishes. Closed Saturday, Sunday and public holidays.

OLD LISBON AND ALFAMA

Casa do Leão ✪✪✪ *Castelo de São Jorge, 1100 Lisbon; Tel. 87 59 62.* A fine restaurant located just inside the castle ramparts and serving a wide range of traditional international and Portuguese dishes. Excellent views. Open daily for lunch only.

O Faz Figura ✪✪✪ *Rua do Paraiso 15B, 1100 Lisbon; Tel. 886 89 81.* Very close to Santa Apolónia station, this restaurant is known for its simple, rustic decor and good atmosphere. Enjoy the traditional local and seafood specialities in these pleasant surroundings. Outdoor dining throughout the summer is a must. Closed Sunday.

Lautasco ✪ *7 Beco do Azinhal, 1100 Lisbon; Tel. 86 10 73.* This restaurant is best known for its pleasant outdoor dining in a simple, shaded courtyard. A variety of good, wholesome food is served in very relaxed and informal surroundings.

Michel ✪✪✪ *Largo de Santa Cruz do Castelo 5, 1100 Lisbon; Tel. 886 43 38.* Next to the Castelo de São Jorge, this restaurant serves a wide range of French, international and Portuguese dishes, and often has folk music in the evenings. Closed Saturday lunchtime, Sunday and public holidays, and in August.

NORTH LISBON

Antonio ✪✪ *Rua Tómas Ribeiro 63, 1000 Lisbon; Tel. 353 87 80.* Situated on the east side of Edward VII Park, this restaurant serves a wide variety of tasty Portuguese and international food.

Antonio Clara – Clube de Empresários ✪✪✪ *Avenida da República 38, 1000 Lisbon. Tel. 796 63 80.* For a more formal atmosphere try this restaurant which is well known for its variety of exquisite French and international dishes.

Magnificently housed in a stylish art nouveau palace. Closed Sunday and last two weeks in August.

Celta ✪ *Rua Gomes Freire 148-C and D, 1100 Lisbon; Tel. 57 30 69.* Typical Portuguese seafood and local dishes. Closed Sunday.

Chez Armand ✪ *Rua Carlos Mardel 38, 1900 Lisbon; Tel. 847 57 70.* Located east of the city centre and serving simple, tasty French cuisine. Closed Saturday lunchtime, Sunday and August.

Clara ✪✪✪ *Campo dos Mártires da Patria 49, 1100 Lisboa; Tel. 885 30 53.* A range of Portuguese and French food is served in this marvellous 18th-century manor house. Outdoor dining is often accompanied by music in the evening. Closed Saturday lunchtime and Sunday.

A Góndola ✪✪ *Avenida de Berna 64, 1000 Lisbon; Tel. 797 04 26.* Outdoor dining in the summer, in a beautiful house situated near the Gulbenkian Museum. Featuring a variety of Italian and local dishes. Closed Saturday evening, Sunday and public holidays.

BELÉM

O Caseiro ✪ *Rua de Belém 35, 1300 Lisbon; Tel. 363 88 03.* In a convenient location between the Coach Museum and the monastery, this is an informal but intimate restaurant serving simple but tasty local dishes. Specialities include porco á alentejana. Closed Sunday and throughout August.

O Rafael ✪ *rua de Belém 106, 1300 Lisbon; Tel. 363 74 20.* Cheap and cheerful, this friendly restaurant is conveniently located near the Monument to the Discoveries. Simple menu offering typical Portuguese fare.

São Jerónimo ✪✪ *Rua dos Jerónimos 12, 1400 Lisbon; Tel. 364 87 96.* Traditional seafood and other local Portuguese dishes in a stylish setting near the Mosteiro dos Jerónimos. Closed Sunday.